L.A. PRIVATE EYES

QUICK TAKES: MOVIES AND POPULAR CULTURE

Quick Takes: Movies and Popular Culture is a series offering suc-
cinct overviews and high-quality writing on cutting-edge themes
and issues in film studies. Authors offer both fresh perspectives
on new areas of inquiry and original takes on established topics.

SERIES EDITORS:

Gwendolyn Audrey Foster is Willa Cather Professor of English
and teaches film studies in the Department of English at the University of Nebraska, Lincoln.

Wheeler Winston Dixon is the James Ryan Endowed Professor of Film Studies and professor of English at the University of
Nebraska, Lincoln.

Rebecca Bell-Metereau, *Transgender Cinema*
Blair Davis, *Comic Book Movies*
Steven Gerrard, *The Modern British Horror Film*
Barry Keith Grant, *Monster Cinema*
Daniel Herbert, *Film Remakes and Franchises*
Ian Olney, *Zombie Cinema*
Valérie K. Orlando, *New African Cinema*
Stephen Prince, *Digital Cinema*
Dahlia Schweitzer, *L.A. Private Eyes*
Steven Shaviro, *Digital Music Videos*
David Sterritt, *Rock 'n' Roll Movies*
John Wills, *Disney Culture*

L.A. Private Eyes

DAHLIA SCHWEITZER

RUTGERS UNIVERSITY PRESS

New Brunswick, Camden, and Newark, New Jersey, and London

Library of Congress Cataloging-in-Publication Data
Names: Schweitzer, Dahlia, author.
Title: L.A. private eyes / Dahlia Schweitzer.
Other titles: LA private eyes | Los Angeles private eyes
Description: New Brunswick : Rutgers University Press, [2019] |
Series: Quick takes: movies and popular culture
Identifiers: LCCN 2018028854 | ISBN 9780813596372 (cloth) |
ISBN 9780813596365 (paperback)
Subjects: LCSH: Detective and mystery stories, American—
History and criticism. | Film noir—United States—History
and criticism. | Detective and mystery television programs—
History and criticism. | Los Angeles (Calif.)—In literature. |
Los Angeles (Calif.)—In motion pictures. | Los Angeles (Calif.)—
On television.
Classification: LCC PS374.D4 S394 2019 |
DDC 813/.087209979494—dc23
LC record available at https://lccn.loc.gov/2018028854

A British Cataloging-in-Publication record for this book is
available from the British Library.

∞ The paper used in this publication meets the requirements of
the American National Standard for Information Sciences—
Permanence of Paper for Printed Library Materials,
ANSI Z39.48-1992.

www.rutgersuniversitypress.org

Manufactured in the United States of America

CONTENTS

CONTENTS

L.A. PRIVATE EYES

INTRODUCTION

I grew up first with Encyclopedia Brown. Then there were Nancy Drew and the Hardy Boys and Tom Swift. I never had much interest in the Bobbsey Twins, but I devoured Miss Marple and Hercule Poirot and Sherlock Holmes. I visited the infamous 221B Baker Street, a miniature Disneyland for mystery buffs. While I adored all the mysteries and took infinite comfort in the reassurance of every tidy ending, the narratives all took place in an imaginary location. The stories always felt like yarns spun by clever authors, intellectual hopscotch to be played on a lazy weekend.

When I moved to Los Angeles, my love of mysteries took on another dimension. I embraced Mickey Haller and Harry Bosch. I tore through Michael Connelly books, discovering the streets of Los Angeles as his characters drove down them, experiencing traffic and crime (and Hollywood, Echo Park, and Van Nuys) through the eyes of Haller and Bosch. These did not feel like imaginary detectives in hypothetical locales. These were real people who were my actual neighbors. Los Angeles became synonymous with crime and intrigue, webs of conspiracy lurking just behind the palm trees and movie stars.

I revisited my favorite film noirs—*Sunset Boulevard, Double Indemnity, The Big Sleep, Chinatown*—and it made sense that they were all in Los Angeles. After all, Los Angeles was the city of crime, belonging to private detectives in trench coats and fedoras, alienated characters imprisoned by the diagonal lines of harsh sunlight on venetian blinds, Cadillacs driving down rain-slicked streets, femmes fatales smoking endless cigarettes in dark alleyways, lit only by the light of the moon. This was my Los Angeles.

What about Jennifer Aniston and Julia Roberts, Robert Downey Jr. and George Clooney? They existed in the same sort of hypothetical imaginary where Miss Marple and Poirot also set up camp, some vague "over there" that was never "here," a fantasy land with a direct conveyer belt to movie theaters and television screens. They were not real, and they were certainly not my neighbors. But Mickey Haller? I was surprised that I did not run into him in the courthouse when I had jury duty.

Los Angeles was the private detective. The private detective was Los Angeles.

I appreciated that mine was not the "normal" Los Angeles, at least not as defined by *TMZ* or the *Hollywood Reporter*. I grew curious as to why, exactly, the private

detective and Los Angeles were so intrinsically intertwined. It was not just the connection between noir and
Los Angeles—a connection that made sense while still
seeming contradictory—or the connection between
Hollywood and the darkness that surrounded the unlucky
actor or actress, such as Lana Turner or Elizabeth Short
(more commonly remembered as the Black Dahlia).
There was something specific about Los Angeles and the
private eye, but I could not put my finger on it.

I watched *The Lincoln Lawyer* (Brad Furman, 2011) and
thought of *Chinatown* (Roman Polanski, 1974). I watched
Chinatown and thought of *The Big Sleep* (Howard Hawks,
1946). I watched *The Big Sleep* and thought of *L.A. Confidential* (Curtis Hanson, 1997). I watched *L.A. Confidential*
and thought of *Devil in a Blue Dress* (Carl Franklin, 1995).
I realized that, as much as the superficial context had
changed, there remained something consistent about the
figure of the L.A. private eye. There was something specific about the way he drove, about the way he understood
the city, and there was something peculiar that happened
when the he was a she.

This book serves as an introduction to the world of the
L.A. private eye. It starts in chapter 1 with an analysis of
place, unpacking the significance of the sprawling streets,
the endless neighborhoods, and the ubiquitous palm
tree. Los Angeles is a place unlike any other, and for this

reason, the L.A. private eye cannot exist anywhere else. Chapter 2 examines the structure of the mystery story, the rules that remain stubbornly consistent over the decades, and the careful motivation and methodology behind this (virtually) unwavering template. Chapter 3 looks at the character of the private detective, his quirks and his talents, the aspects of who he is that make him so uniquely suited to this city by the sea. Chapters 4–6 explore what happens when the private detective is "different," when he is no longer the ordinary white man who can blend in so easily in Brentwood and Silver Lake, in courthouses and city halls. While the conventions of the genre may have remained consistent and recognizable, the points where they evolve illuminate much about our changing gender and power roles. What happens when the private eye is no longer white? No longer a man? No longer an adult? These chapters examine the various ways the archetype has been both challenged and redefined. Finally, the book considers how we might be moving toward a version 2.0, a new private eye better suited to the world in which we currently live than Philip Marlowe, a legend, to be sure, but also an artifact of the past.

1

LOS ANGELES

L.A. has always been flat and featureless. Anybody could be anywhere out there. . . . There was no logic to the layout of the city. And there were more people every day. Sharecroppers and starlets, migrant Mexicans and insurance salesman, come to pick over the money tree for a few years before they went home. But they never went home.   —Walter Mosley, *Black Betty*

THE L.A. PRIVATE EYE

From Raymond Chandler's Philip Marlowe to Michael Connelly's "Lincoln Lawyer" (aka Mickey Haller), the figure of the renegade sleuth driving around the winding, crime-ridden streets of L.A. has remained a favorite for almost a century. Permanently single, often alcoholic, usually en route to emphysema, and always acting alone, the L.A. private eye has become an icon. And the rootlessness of his footsteps—rarely would we find him in a permanent place of his own—echoed that of many Angelinos.

The detective's home would inevitably become a surrogate office space, and his office space would be his car. Humphrey Bogart as Philip Marlowe in *The Big Sleep* (Howard Hawks, 1946) may have shaped the mold, giving us the lasting visual of the trench-coated private eye with rain dripping from the brim of his hat, but detectives have continued to roam the streets of Los Angeles as solitary heroes and urban knights ever since. Despite the rapid evolution of society since the 1930s, the conventions of the genre, the character of our hero, and the trappings of the city have remained consistent.

Surprisingly, considering the power and persistence of that enigmatic figure known colloquially as the "L.A. private eye," or P.I. (private investigator), he is a relatively recent creation. Not even a hundred years old, he first appeared on the pages of Raymond Chandler's novel *The Big Sleep* in 1939. *The Big Sleep* was then adapted into the classic film—starring Humphrey Bogart as the quintessential L.A. private eye—seven years later, not only shaping the template of the L.A. private eye but also embracing and advancing the aesthetic and tone of "film noir."

NOIR

Literally translating to "black film," film noir was only referred to as such in later years. At the time of the initial release of noir films, they were merely considered to be melodramas. French film critics, however, finally able to watch Hollywood pictures again after World War II, observed the distinctive darkness—both literal and metaphorical—of films such as *The Big Sleep*, *The Maltese Falcon* (John Huston, 1941), *Double Indemnity* (Billy Wilder, 1944), *Laura* (Otto Preminger, 1944), and *Murder, My Sweet* (Edward Dmytryk, 1944). The French critic Nino Frank may have coined the term "film noir" in 1946, but the term was not adopted in America until the 1960s and '70s. It then came to refer to films made in America largely during the 1940s and 1950s that had a style both dark and cynical, with urban settings full of pessimism, fatalism, and paranoia and characters full of intrigue and suspicion.

Visually, the high-contrast black-and-white imagery echoed the cinematography common to German expressionism, a German art and film movement characterized by highly dramatic visuals and psychological states. These films often featured criminals, psychopaths, and serial killers, such as the character of Jack the Ripper (Gustav Diessl) in Georg Pabst's *Pandora's Box* (1929) or Hans Beckert (Peter Lorre) in Fritz Lang's *M* (1931). Many German filmmakers, such as Lang, Billy Wilder, and Otto Preminger, came to Hollywood to escape the Nazi regime, and they brought this style with them. As David

Marsham wrote for *Life* magazine in 1947, "Whoever went to the movies with any regularity during 1946 was caught in the middle of Hollywood's profound postwar affection for morbid drama. From January through December, deep shadows, clutching hands, exploding revolvers, sadistic villains and heroines tormented with deeply rooted diseases of the mind flashed across the screen in a panting display of psychoneuroses, unsublimated sex and murder most foul" (qtd. in Clarens 192). While this comment may be as melodramatic as some of the plot twists found onscreen, it does reflect the popularity of noir films and the vivid imagery within then.

More than just a group of films particular to a certain era, noir became a style, a reflection of urban anxiety that transcended a specific moment in time. The protagonists of these movies—much like the character of the private detective—were defined by an inability "to dwell comfortably anywhere" (Dimendberg 7). Aimless, violent, perpetually on the outside of every official institution, these were true antiheroes, seemingly just as prone to violence as to acts of integrity. The films would inevitably revolve around a male protagonist—bitter, jaded, and down on his luck—who would be seduced by a femme fatale with ulterior motives. She would betray him, and there would often be at least one fatality, if not a threat to the protagonist to give up and go home (wherever that might be). The story lines were usually complex and disorienting, with lots of flashbacks and plot twists, while the endings were rarely optimistic. The disorientation was enhanced visually, as well, with the use of techniques such as multiple reflections—rendering it difficult to determine which image was "real"—and shots through curved or frosted glass. A sense of claustrophobia or entrapment was a must, usually enhanced by the prison-bar-like shadows of window blinds and the frequent darkness lurking at the edge of every frame. It was often raining, and there was frequent use of voice-over.

Even though not all noir films contained private detectives—*Double Indemnity* features an insurance claims investigator, and *Touch of Evil* features both a Mexican drug enforcement official and some American police officers, for instance—others such as *The Maltese Falcon* (based on the novel of the same name by Dashiell Hammett), *The Big Sleep* (based on the novel of the same name by Raymond Chandler), *Murder, My Sweet* (based on Raymond Chandler's novel *Farewell, My Lovely* and also featuring Philip Marlowe, only this time played by Dick Powell), and *Kiss Me Deadly* (Robert Aldrich, 1955) helped to craft the iconic character. And all but *The Maltese Falcon* (which is set in San Francisco) and *Touch of Evil* (which is set on the Mexican-U.S. border) are set in Los Angeles.

Raymond Chandler wrote seven novels set in Los Angeles. All were turned into films, some more than once. Chandler also worked on the screenplays for *Double Indemnity*, *The Blue Dahlia* (George Marshall, 1946), and *Strangers on a Train* (Alfred Hitchcock, 1951). But the film that both defined the noir style and launched the character of the private detective was the first film adaptation of *The Big Sleep*, directed by Howard Hawks and starring Humphrey Bogart and Lauren Bacall. Both the book and the film set up a stark contrast between the enormous mansion belonging to General Sternwood (Charles Waldron) up in the luxurious hills and the shadier parts of Los Angeles below, complete with gamblers, pornographers, nymphomaniacs, and illicit homosexual relationships. The story revolves around the general and his two daughters, Carmen (Martha Vickers) and Vivian (Bacall). The bookseller Arthur Geiger (Theodore von Eltz), a man who claims that Carmen owes him money, is blackmailing Sternwood. Sternwood hires private detective Philip Marlowe (Bogart) to take care of the problem. Marlowe discovers that Geiger is actually running an illegal pornography operation out of the bookstore. At this point, the plot becomes notoriously complicated; additional bodies surface, someone gets poisoned, and other people are shot. Marlowe has more questions than answers when he discovers that Vivian is also being blackmailed and

Vivian's husband, Regan, mysteriously disappears. Vivian has gambling debts, although hers are owed to Eddie Mars (John Ridgely), and, unsurprisingly, attempts are made on Marlowe's life. This complexity is common to these types of stories, in which the actual initial crime proves only a buoy marking the sordid depths just beneath.

Marlowe eventually realizes that nothing will ever really change and that the rich will never pay for their crimes. Whereas in the book Carmen suffers no penalty for her actions—including killing Regan and trying to kill Marlowe—the Production Code officials insisted that the film version provide more of a punishment for her sins, and Carmen is sent to an asylum or rehabilitation institution to be "cured." General Sternwood, however, is told lies about the events in order to appease him. This lack of resolution or restitution is common to narratives in which the goal for the private eye is never to vanquish "the bad guys" but merely to maintain some form of stoic integrity, to protect those who need protecting—while wading through the sordid muck.

Told as a series of episodic scenes rather than one overarching narrative, *The Big Sleep*—both the film and the book—can be hard to follow. In fact, Chandler himself recounts a time when Hawks and Bogart "got into an argument as to whether one of the characters was murdered or committed suicide": "They sent me a wire ... and dammit

I didn't know either" ("Letter to Jamie Hamilton" 105). Chandler did not know because these "minor" details do not matter. The purpose of the detective narrative, as seen in *The Big Sleep*, is merely to present these episodic fragments; life is portrayed as a series of moments without an overarching narrative. It is the crime that becomes the impromptu organizational device, not only in *The Big Sleep* but in other detective narratives to follow. The crime provides an illusion of movement to a string of otherwise plotless moments, organizing those moments "into the formally satisfying arabesques of a puzzle unfolding," writes Fredric Jameson, in his book *Raymond Chandler: The Detections of Totality*. Jameson goes on to emphasize, however, that the puzzle is a mere distraction from the real content of these narratives: the setting (6). And the setting that would inevitably be linked to the iconic private detective is the city of Los Angeles.

Los Angeles, as depicted by Chandler, is a city full of desire and deceit, where money, power, and ambition hold more ground than morality, law, or tradition, where bookstores conceal pornography and private mansions conceal murder. And it is the drive to penetrate the mask, to discover the truth behind the façade, to expose the secrets that would otherwise remain hidden that drives both the L.A. detective and the L.A. detective story. This is why both belong together.

LOS ANGELES

Unexpectedly, for a city known for sunshine and sprawl, noir was defined by Los Angeles, and Los Angeles was defined by noir. The real-life characteristics of Los Angeles—the endless winding roads, the sudden cliffs and breathtaking views, the waves beating against the shore, the rows of palm trees, the Hollywood glitterati with their sordid secrets, the Spanish-style architecture—became intertwined with the noir aesthetic. The urban form offered by Los Angeles is markedly different from the urban form of Manhattan. This allowed Los Angeles to become the ultimate example of a city sans center, a perfect setting for a protagonist who cannot find his way home. The aimless sprawl, the insular nature of specific neighborhoods, and the fundamental incomprehensibility of the city became repeated themes in film noir as well as in detective narratives—in film, television, and books.

Not only was the verticality of New York superseded by the horizontal nature of Los Angeles, the claustrophobia of Manhattan replaced by seemingly endless urban sprawl, but the jostling crowds of midtown were exchanged for the isolation of a car. Nowhere became as defined by the automobile as Los Angeles. In keeping with the Department of City Planning's 1941 regional parkway model, which ordained the car as its centerpiece, the car became the pivot around which Los Angeles revolved. Representing a shifting U.S. economy, one that swapped a principally rural country with the highway, Los Angeles offered a visual manifestation of a faster, more stream-lined way of life. The success of the Arroyo Seco Parkway, built between Los Angeles and Pasadena in 1940, encour-aged the construction of a massive freeway network. (Cal-ifornia was unique in insisting that highways be called "freeways," despite just how "free" that highway might become at rush hour.) This network promised to alleviate growing congestion within the Los Angeles metropolitan area and to connect Los Angeles to outlying cities such as Whittier and Long Beach, as well as to improve rates of home ownership. Proximity to a city center was no longer as desirable as a house in the suburbs, and Los Angeles was desperate to demonstrate that this was the case. Con-struction on this freeway network began in the early 1950s and was mostly finished by the mid-1960s, shaping Los Angeles for decades to come.

Any sense of a central urban community was now re-placed by freeway exits, pockets of internally defined areas that separated the larger city into isolated neighbor-hoods. As Norman M. Klein writes in his book *The His-tory of Forgetting: Los Angeles and the Erasure of Memory*, "One literally passes through to arrive, but rarely stops. We are supposed to watch, or be watched, in the privacy of our vehicle" (85). This isolation was reinforced by the anonymity of transportation, people making lonely commutes in their pod-like automobiles. No matter how crowded the streets or freeways, Angelinos remained alone, albeit colored by the neighborhoods they traversed or failed to leave. Los Angeles became distinguished not only by the automobile but also by these seemingly different and distinct spaces that lived cheek by jowl, a characteristic integral to the development of the L.A. private eye.

Los Angeles had more problems than traffic and isolation, however. Despite the efforts of the lush landscaping to conceal the fact, Los Angeles is a desert, and this means that it is a city under constant pressure to maintain a water supply. By 1904, the population of Los Angeles had increased from eleven thousand in 1880 to above two hundred thousand. Water—or the lack thereof—became a pressing concern. William Mulholland, superintendent of a private water company that was purchased by the city in 1904, found water 250 miles north, on the edge of the High Sierras, in Owens Valley (Eaton 24). The city of Los Angeles began buying up more and more land and water rights from Owens Valley, even filing suit in 1924 against some of the valley's farmers for "wrongfully diverting" the water into their own irrigation ditches. Despite continued protests from Owens Valley residents, Mulholland built the Los Angeles Aqueduct to divert water from the Owens

Valley region to the growing metropolis. The farmers' response was to blow up a spillway gate with dynamite. Over the next three years, "at least seven more blasts damaged the northern end of the aqueduct" (Malnic). City employees would be held at gunpoint and chased out of Owens Valley when they were recognized. Eventually the residents of Owens Valley gave up, leaving Los Angeles to pretend it had always had its own water supply. This particular narrative formed the basis for the classic L.A. private eye film *Chinatown* (Roman Polanski, 1974).

There was more to shatter the illusion of paradise by the sea. During the 1920s, the population of Los Angeles continued to rise dramatically as a result of the discovery of oil. However, as thousands made their way west, dreaming of financial success and lucrative possibility, they were met, instead, with high prices and low salaries. The lack of employment led to tensions between new residents, established residents, and ethnic minorities who were seen as competition for a limited number of jobs. While conflicts between white military personnel and police officers on the one hand and Latino and African Americans on the other was nothing new, these tensions were fueled further by poor working conditions for Mexicans, persistently inflammatory and derogatory language by the press, and building developments that displaced Hispanic neighborhoods.

In June 1943, eleven sailors in downtown Los Angeles got into an altercation with a group of Mexican youth. This altercation prompted thousands of military personnel, off-duty police, and civilians to beat up and arrest more than five hundred Latino and African American youth. Referred to as the "Zoot Suit Riots," in response to the suits popular among these youth, the racial tensions had nothing to do with apparel. However, those who wore the flashy suits—often accessorized with porkpie hats and watch chains—were frequently assumed to be dangerous criminals and were described as such by the media. Rioting spread throughout Los Angeles, with taxi drivers fuelling the fire by offering servicemen free rides to rioting areas. Military personnel and civilians from around Southern California streamed toward Los Angeles, eager to beat up Mexicans, Filipinos, and African Americans. The riots only subsided when U.S. military personnel were confined to their base, Los Angeles declared off-limits (Andrews). This was only a temporary fix, however, as the racial tensions would simmer for decades to come.

With the city's combination of "anything goes" mentality and get-rich-quick aspirations, Los Angeles also became an example of sordid living and corruption. As David Fine describes in his book *Imagining Los Angeles*, L.A. was "a big city layered on a Wild West frontier town," and behind the scenes was "a corrupt municipal government." Fine describes gangsters and gamblers, drug addicts and prostitutes, all part of a web of collusion and scandal that rocked not only the big local industries—oil and movies—but plenty of others along the way. Everything was for sale, including police protection (118). Mob activity in Los Angeles began around the start of the century, and the mob was often involved with anything involving trucks or truckers in Hollywood. It was also common for mobsters, moguls, and movie stars to commingle, crossing paths at "nightclubs, bars, clandestine gambling establishments, and private parties," their interactions often including alcohol, drugs, prostitution, gambling, and blackmail (Lewis 52). In 1950, the Los Angeles Police Department seized a personal phone book belonging to Mickey Cohen, an American gangster who had moved to Los Angeles to work under "Bugsy" Siegel. Contact information for a variety of Hollywood celebrities, including Frank Sinatra, Milton Berle, Joan Collins, Humphrey Bogart, and Lauren Bacall, was included in this book, revealing just how commonplace interactions had become between ruthless gangers and movie stars (Lewis 69, 208n27).

The discovery of Elizabeth Short's body in January 1947 helped mark the shift from a Hollywood where everything seemed possible to a Hollywood that was brutal and unforgiving. The still-unsolved murder of

Short—an aspiring actress who had moved to Los Angeles to pursue a career as an actress and who came to be known posthumously as the "Black Dahlia"—was the first in a series of murders that cemented Hollywood's reputation as a place replete with crime and corruption, a reputation reinforced by the mobsters and transients who also became synonymous with the movie industry. The very next month, a bulldozer operator reporting for work discovered the mutilated body of Jeanne French, and Evelyn Winters was found strangled and beaten to death in March 1947. Even though there was speculation that the same person had killed all three women, there was never any conclusive proof. As Jon Lewis writes, in his book *Hard-Boiled Hollywood: Crime and Punishment in Postwar Los Angeles*, Short's death stood as "a metonymy for a generation of young women whose dreams were dashed on the streets of the city," having imagined "a place that no longer existed" (12, 15). The death of Marilyn Monroe fifteen years later further tarnished the image of Hollywood as a city of possibility and glamour, reminding everyone that darkness lurked beneath the surface.

Hollywood, especially, became known for crime and self-obsession, for embodying the worst side effects of ambition and greed. Originally published in Paris in 1959, Kenneth Anger's infamous book *Hollywood Babylon: The Legendary Underground Classic of Hollywood's Darkest and Best Kept Secrets* was published in America in 1965, banned ten days later, and then rereleased in 1975. In the book, Anger describes the sleazy secrets of Hollywood's well-known stars, linking the movie industry to sex scandals, drug overdoses, and alcoholism. While *Hollywood Babylon* may have intermixed fiction with fact, the sterile and perfectly poised image of Hollywood had been shattered, replaced by a fascination with what lay beneath and beyond the silver screen.

In *L.A. Confidential*, Sid Hudgens (Danny DeVito) is the publisher of *Hush-Hush*, a tabloid magazine specializing in celebrity gossip and other exposés about Hollywood scandals. Hudgens's catchphrase, with which he ends most of his articles, is "Off the record, on the QT, and very hush-hush." Notably, the last two—*On the QT* and *Hush-Hush*—as well as *Confidential* were names of actual scandal sheets. In fact, the tag line for *Confidential* was "Uncensored and Off the Record," while the tag line for *Hush-Hush* was "What You Don't Know About People You Know."

This notion of "What You Don't Know About People You Know" translates quite literally into the myth-making machine of Hollywood. As Hudgens declares in the film's opening voice-over, "Come to Los Angeles. There are jobs aplenty and land is cheap. Life is good in Los Angeles. It's paradise on earth, but there's trouble in paradise. The head of organized crime in these parts runs dope, rackets, and prostitution. How can organized crime exist in the city with the best police force in the world?" The reality is that the captain of the "best police force in the world" is moving to take over from the former head of organized crime, Mickey Cohen (Paul Guilfoyle), after Cohen is imprisoned for tax evasion. But this is only part of the irony that makes up Los Angeles and only a small part of the irony that makes up *L.A. Confidential*.

Hudgens goes on: "Come to Los Angeles! The sun shines bright, the beaches are wide and inviting, and the orange groves stretch as far as the eye can see. There are jobs aplenty, and land is cheap. Every working man can have his own house, and inside every house, a happy all-American family. You can have all this! And who knows? You could even be discovered ... become a movie star! Or at least see one. Life is good in Los Angeles. . . . It's paradise on Earth." But then he laughs. "That's what they tell ya anyway. Because they're selling an image. They're selling it through movies, radio, and television." Not only are they selling something that looks like paradise (but is actually quite the opposite), but *L.A. Confidential* also features prostitutes who look like classic Hollywood actresses. Via makeup, hair dye, and plastic surgery, a group of women have been turned into celluloid fantasies made real, even if the resemblance is barely skin deep. What better metaphor could describe the Hollywood industry?

During the 1940s and 1950s, Hollywood was rocked by the actions of Senator Joseph McCarthy and the House Un-American Activities Committee (HUAC). An investigative committee of the United States House of Representatives, the HUAC was formed in 1938 ostensibly to investigate potential Communist ties among American citizens and organizations. Senator McCarthy, as chairman of the Government Operations Committee, claimed that Communist spies and sympathizers had infiltrated Hollywood studios, as well as the federal government. Thus encouraged, the HUAC blacklisted more than three hundred Hollywood directors, actors, and screenwriters in 1947, causing them to be deemed unhireable by the studios. While some continued to work under fake names, many were unable to find future employment in Hollywood.

Despite the relentless sunshine of Los Angeles—and the perfectly packaged gloss of Hollywood—events such as the publication of *Hollywood Babylon*, the HUAC blacklist, the aqueduct bombings, and the Zoot Suit Riots demonstrate the dark and ugly underside to the sunny Southern California fantasy. These themes, combined with the magnetic appeal of gangsters, femmes fatales, and corrupt politicians, filled the pages of pulp paperbacks and national newspapers, as well as inspiring count-less films and television shows. In these narratives, Los Angeles—and Hollywood in particular—was depicted as a pretty face masking a hotbed of crime and corruption, a perpetual swarm of evil and decay just waiting to be exposed. This Los Angeles was full of shadows and fog, rain permanently glinting in the moonlight, and criminals lurking around every corner. Los Angeles, as depicted in movies such as *The Big Sleep* and *Double Indemnity*, was this place, in marked contrast to the stereotypical "always sunny" image of the city.

And when the city is actually sunny, the perfection of the weather only heightens the contrast between the illusion of Hollywood and the crime and corruption hap-pening underneath its glamorous veneer. Early in *L.A. Confidential,* Bud White (Russell Crowe) approaches a house decked out in Christmas lights. Despite the cheerful sled and reindeer on the house's roof, White can hear the husband shouting at his wife from the street. The abusive language and tears within the house are jarringly out of place with the decorations outside it. The scene takes place at night, of course, so as to display the twinkling Christmas lights. To further hit home the odd juxtaposition of the scene, the wife wishes White a merry Christmas after he handcuffs her husband to the porch.

This fascination with L.A. as a hotbed of crime and corruption barely concealed by the palm trees and blond bombshells proved to be an integral component in the private eye narrative. Unlike the tales of granny sleuths, such as Jessica Fletcher (Angela Lansbury) on *Murder, She Wrote* (CBS, 1983–1996) or Agatha Christie's Miss Marple, in which crime is a horrific anomaly to be corrected, solved, and tucked away like a bad dream, in Los Angeles, crime is constant. Each specific case becomes an excuse to expose the hidden corruption or wrongdoing. This is why crimes (and criminals) are rarely simple in L.A. detective narratives. They are the metaphoric equivalent of a loose thread that, when you tug on it, causes the whole sweater to unravel. What seems at first to be a simple murder, kidnapping, or blackmail is inevitably linked to political corruption or criminal conspiracy on a massive scale. These narratives depict a world where nobody is as he or she appears, and everyone is an unreliable narrator, omniscient or otherwise. While there is satisfaction coming from the eventual reveal, from the illusion that logic and order are (temporarily) restored, there is also no pretense that the detective has vanquished crime and criminality. They will only continue somewhere else, at some other time, at the hands of yet another shadowy figure.

Not only does Los Angeles offer a dizzying range of crime and criminals, but it also was, and still is, a city divided by wealth. As depicted in *The Big Sleep*, the very rich live in the hills, up curving driveways, while the very poor live in the sprawling flatlands down below. Film noir often explores the sharp differences between those who had money and those who did not. Mansions are opulent and brightly lit, whereas cheap bars and dirty apartments are dark and decrepit. The only person who can easily transition from one neighborhood to the other, regardless of race and social class, is the private detective, the new urban cowboy. Viewers and readers need him to guide them through an urban environment that grows more menacing, more overwhelming, and more isolating by the day. They need his eyes and his automobile in order to experience and understand the city as a whole.

Appropriately, Marlowe moves between the very rich and the very poor, neither above violence or afraid to use it, but never taking more than "twenty-five dollars a day and expenses." As an errant knight, Marlowe is in dogged pursuit of righting wrongs—but he is also willing to perform the occasional wrong along the way if doing so would serve the greater good. We follow him in this pursuit, limited to his point of view for our understandings of the events that transpire. He is our eyes and our ears.

Frank McShane, noted for his biography *The Life of Raymond Chandler*, writes that there is "something appropriate in Chandler's choosing the detective story as his vehicle for presenting Los Angeles" (66). In contrast to traditional detective narratives, which revolve around a limited cast of characters in a limited number of settings, the new form of the detective story was intrinsically suited to a city like Los Angeles and, as such, involves "an extraordinary range of humanity, from the very rich to the very poor, and can encompass a great many different places" (McShane 66–67). Los Angeles is a city built on extremes.

One of the reasons why Los Angeles is able to contain so many extremes is because of its massive size. With an area of just over five hundred square miles, Los Angeles dwarfs every other metropolitan region in the United States. Because of this massive size, and the dizzying number of people within, it makes perfect sense that one of the fundamental qualities of the hardboiled detective is his ability not only to drive through the countless neighborhoods that make up the L.A. region but to make sense of them and their inhabitants. In contrast, a typical old-fashioned mystery plot is a murder in a house, the suspects confined to that house until their gradual elimination reveals the criminal. This format was repeatedly demonstrated by Nick and Nora Charles, a fictional married couple created by Dashiell Hammett in his novel *The Thin Man*. In the original novel, published in 1934, as well as in the films, radio broadcasts, television programs, and theatrical productions that followed, the adventures of this bickering and lighthearted duo follow this familiar template. It is impossible to imagine Nick and Nora, much less J. B. Fletcher or Miss Marple, hanging up a shingle in Los Angeles.

There are other reasons why Los Angeles is uniquely suited to the hardboiled private eye. For instance, its physical proximity to the Pacific Ocean offers a tantalizing refuge from a land increasingly "polluted and despoiled" (Porter, *Pursuit* 199). At the same time, the water provides an inflexible border. Ray B. Browne writes that Ross Macdonald chose Los Angeles as the location for his famous Lew Archer detective series because people, with their backs to the sea, were "unable to run any farther," and they would have no choice but "to confront the forces that seemed set to destroy them" (4).

Another supposed allure of Los Angeles and Hollywood is the notion that, among the palm trees and blinding sunshine, one can reinvent oneself, perhaps the ultimate escape. More specifically, Hollywood (and L.A. by proxy) promises the ability to manufacture a new image if you do not like the one you already have. One can go from being Norma Jeane Baker to being Marilyn Monroe, from Archibald Leach to Cary Grant, in the blink of an eye or, better yet, with the stroke of a publicist's pen. However, the detective serves as a reminder that one cannot escape one's past. Even while the L.A. detective story is a response to the freedom and mobility associated with the open road—with "the road that points west, away from the history-bound East and into the open, future-oriented West," a response to the promise of "the new, free, self-made American" (Fine 134)—it also represents absolute limits, with the ocean as the literal end of the road.

In the book *Negative Space: Manny Farber on the Movies*, Manny Farber writes that there are three kinds of film space: the screen itself, on which the celluloid images are projected (or from which the digital images are displayed); the psychological space that exists within the actor's imagination; and the actual physical space within which the narrative unfolds (3). For the L.A. private eye, Los Angeles is both a psychological and a physical space. Los Angeles is where he drives his car, it is where he meets his clients, it is where he stands in the rain for a quick cigarette, and it is where the neon signs glow on his way home. It is where movies are made and where dreams die. It is where anything is possible and everything is fake. It is where everyone drives together and yet remains alone. It is where corruption lurks beneath seemingly omnipresent sun. It is both too bright and too dark. It is where everything seems perfect—but nothing is, if you look closely enough.

2

THE DETECTIVE STORY

Next to the western, the hard-boiled detective story is
America's most distinctive contribution to the world's
stock of action-adventure stories.

—John Cawelti, "*Chinatown* and Generic
Transformation in Recent American Films"

THE EARLY DAYS

Edgar Allan Poe is commonly considered to have written the first mystery tale with his "Murders in the Rue
Morgue," published in *Graham's Magazine* in 1841. However, a likely inspiration for him was E. T. A. Hoffman's
novella *Mademoiselle de Scudéri*, published in 1819 and a
critical and commercial success. In Hoffman's novella,
the city of Paris is reeling from thefts of high-end jewelry
made by the goldsmith René Cardillac. While some of
the victims are merely knocked unconscious, others have
been killed. When Cardillac himself is found dead, his
apprentice, Olivier Brusson, is immediately charged with

the crime. However, Cardillac's daughter, who is in love with the apprentice, insists that he is innocent. She convinces Mademoiselle de Scudéri to investigate. Scudéri eventually discovers that Cardillac himself was responsible for the thefts and the murders and that a member of the royal guard had killed him. The plot device of the solitary investigator working against the convictions or interests of the police department is especially notable. This device has been repurposed time and time again for the hard-boiled detective narrative.

Published about twenty years later, Poe's "Murders in the Rue Morgue" begins with a description of the term "ratiocination," commonly defined as the process of exact thinking or reasoning. In this case, the character of amateur detective C. Augustin Dupin—who first appeared in "Murders in the Rue Morgue" but would return for Poe's "The Mystery of Marie Roget," published in *Ladies' Companion* in 1842, and "The Purloined Letter," published in *The Gift* for 1844—uses ratiocination to solve crimes. Poe offers an explanation of the term using the example of a chess player. Being a good chess player is not merely about being a good observer or having a good memory, he writes. Instead, it is about "the quality of the observation. The necessary knowledge is that of *what* to observe." A good chess player will note "every variation of face as the play progresses, gathering a fund of thought from the differences in the expression of certainty, of surprise, of triumph, or of chagrin" (Poe 82, 83). Similarly, the private detective builds his case with observations that would elude the ordinary mortal. In fact, Dupin is so gifted at putting himself in the mind of the criminal that he can appear to be an actual mind reader.

Dupin, along with his unnamed companion (setting the stage for later same-sex sleuthing sidekicks such as Dr. Watson, in the case of Sherlock Holmes, and Captain Hastings, in the case of Hercule Poirot), investigates a series of murders in Poe's three short stories. Dupin's primary motivation is intellectual curiosity but also, in the case of "Murders in the Rue Morgue," to prove the innocence of a wrongfully accused man, much as in *Mademoiselle de Scudéri*.

In "Murders in the Rue Morgue," the wrongfully accused man is Adolphe Le Bon, who had briefly crossed paths with Dupin. Discovering the case in question by reading about it in a newspaper, Dupin decides to offer his services to the police, intrigued by the mysterious murder of a mother and daughter. After careful observation and deduction, Dupin comes to the conclusion that an orangutan committed the bizarre murders. The orangutan in question is found, and Le Bon is released. Neither the orangutan nor his owner is held responsible for the crime, which is deemed to be an unfortunate accident.

This establishes a precedent for the uneasy resolution that also became a frequent trope in later detective stories.

Another precedent established by Poe is the emphasis on the necessary steps taken to solve the mystery at hand. As would be the case in virtually every subsequent detective narrative, the actual crime plays a much smaller part than the action taken to expose and understand it. Other tropes established or reinforced by Poe are the unexpected reveal of a surprise criminal, someone the police did not suspect; the intentional misleading of the police by the real criminal; a bizarre crime taking place in a locked room; and the character of the unusually gifted detective, for whom judicious observation provides the most direct insight to the truth. These tropes have manifested themselves in future mysteries for decades to come.

COZY VERSUS HARD-BOILED

By the end of the nineteenth century, detective stories had steadily increased in popularity in England. There was the launch of Sherlock Holmes by Arthur Conan Doyle in 1887, a hugely popular character who appeared in a total of four novels and fifty-six short stories, and the subsequent success of the mystery authors Agatha Christie, known primarily for her fictional detectives Hercule

Poirot and Miss Marple starting in 1920; Dorothy Say-
ers, creator of the amateur sleuth Lord Peter Wimsey in
1923; and G. K. Chesterton, whose priest-detective Father
Brown was featured in fifty-three short stories published
between 1910 and 1936. The character of Holmes might
be more physically active than Poe's Dupin, but he—like
Poirot, Marple, Wimsey, and Brown—still relies on careful observation and deduction to solve the case. These
depictions of puzzles unfolding, regardless of whether by
a violin-playing eccentric, an elderly spinster, or an obses-
sively tidy Belgian with a memorable mustache, proved
financially viable, to say the least. It is no accident that
Agatha Christie is the best-selling novelist of all time.

These British mysteries—aptly described as "cozy
mysteries"—were very different, however, from the ones
gaining popularity in the United States at the same time.
In the British mysteries, the crime is, most often, a glaring anomaly to the peacefulness of day-to-day existence
that the detective manages to put to rights, efficiently
and satisfyingly, by the close of the narrative. Once the
detective has identified and excised the villain, law and
order returns to the once-peaceful village. Appropriately
enough, the setting for these "cozy mysteries" is usually
as limited as the cast of characters—often a small village,
a train, or even an island—ensuring that the solution be
precise and tidy.

In contrast, the American version of these detective narratives—commonly referred to as "hard-boiled" (quite literally because the stereotypical hard-boiled detective is hard on the outside and soft on the inside)— are anything but cozy and their resolutions anything but tidy. More often than not, settings and characters feel limitless. In fact, the anonymity and urban sprawl of Los Angeles became an essential component.

Not only were space and character different in the American version, but perspective was as well. In the traditional British detective narrative, criminals follow some sort of logical process that enables the detective to unravel the crime through obtaining the necessary information. This is why Poirot and Holmes (along with their contemporaries) are able to use logic—"In the little grey cells of the brain lies the solution to every mystery," Poirot explains (Christie 97)—to deduce not only the identity of the criminal but also the motive and technique. However, as the world confronted World War I, logic and reason felt far less effective. It seemed wildly implausible that one individual, no matter how clever or observant, could restore order with brainpower alone. This bleak new perspective also meant that treating death as an intellectual exercise seemed trivial and even disrespectful. A new style of detective narrative was inevitable.

The end of the nineteenth century also featured a period of tremendous growth for the U.S. publishing industry—facilitated by a rapid expansion in population, as well as a rise in the literacy rate—which encouraged the success of magazines and dime novels. "The Old Sleuth," the first continuously running detective series, was launched in 1872. Created by Harlan Page Halsey, the series initially appeared in *Fireside Companion* magazine before receiving its own publication, the *Old Sleuth Library*. Not old at all, the "Old Sleuth" was a young private eye who disguised himself as an aged man. The series moved to *Old Sleuth Weekly*, where it ran for two hundred issues, from 1908 to 1921 (Walton 162, 163). The success of *Old Sleuth Weekly* led to the creation of other similarly themed magazines, including *Black Mask, Detective Fiction Weekly, Dime Detective, Thrilling Detective, Street & Smith's Detective Stories*, and even *Hollywood Detective*.

The cheap weeklies, magazines, and dime novels (otherwise known as "pulps") did feature other kinds of narratives—including romance and westerns—but the detective story proved the most popular. Readers became acquainted with the tough, street-smart detective who could not be more different than the soft-spoken puzzle solver common to British mysteries. Unlike the more cerebral efforts of Sherlock Holmes and Hercule Poirot, the hard-boiled detective would rarely be found in his office and would even more rarely be found sitting still. Hard-boiled fiction became known for its fast-paced dialogue, its tough protagonists, and its depictions of cities full of crime, sex, violence, and corruption.

Joseph T. Shaw, the most influential editor of *Black Mask*, was a big supporter of this new style of writing, going so far as to specify certain characteristics that would help define this new kind of narrative. He argued on behalf of "simplicity for the sake of clarity, plausibility and belief"; for action involving "recognizable human character"; "authenticity in character and plot"; and "economy of expression" (qtd. in Baker and Nietzel 4). This new kind of narrative would also be defined by a tough protagonist (always male), while women were frequently deceitful and uncooperative. The villains were inevitably rich, corrupt, and/or criminal.

Carroll John Daly, who wrote short stories for *Black Mask*, is credited with helping to shape the mold of the private detective. Daly's New York–based detective, Race Williams, described himself as follows: "The police don't like me. The crooks don't like me. I'm just a halfway house between the law and crime; sort of working both ends against the middle. Right and wrong are not written on the statutes for me, nor do I find my code of morals in the essays of long-winded professors. My ethics are my own" (Daly 11–12). Here we can already see the alienation common to the hard-boiled private eye, the in-between state within which he spends most of his time—never one of the good guys or one of the bad, never part of the crowd, but always somehow acting alone in order to do the right thing. The success of Daly's stories encouraged the editors of *Black Mask* magazine to feature other crime writers with similar detectives, such as Dashiell Hammett, the author of *The Maltese Falcon* and *The Thin Man* and creator of the character Sam Spade. Hammett, in turn, inspired Raymond Chandler and James Cain to try their hand at hard-boiled fiction. It was Chandler and Cain who moved the detective to Los Angeles, a destination that now feels inevitable.

Before too long, these four—Daly, Hammett, Chandler, and Cain—established what we now think of as the American crime story. Not only did they shape the character of the hard-boiled private eye, but they also shaped the stories within which he would exist. They took the mystery out of the living room and put it into the streets, where it became less of an intellectual puzzle to be solved and more of a social commentary, a reflection of real urban life rather than reassuring fantasy. Hammett even used his experiences as an operative for the Pinkerton Detective Agency to lend authenticity to his writing, while Cain—whose novels *The Postman Always Rings Twice, Mildred Pierce,* and *Double Indemnity* were adapted into films—used news headlines and the tabloids as inspiration for his writings.

RADIO AND HOLLYWOOD

In 1930, the detective story hit radio, when the publishers of *Detective Story* magazine hired writers to develop stories from the magazine into a radio-friendly format for the *Detective Story Hour*. During that same decade, the detective story also hit Hollywood—usually through adaptations of the original books—with films such as *The Maltese Falcon* (Roy Del Ruth, 1931), *The Thin Man* (W. S. Van Dyke, 1934), and *Murders in the Rue Morgue* (Robert Florey, 1932). The film adaptation of *The Thin Man*—based on the book by Dashiell Hammett—was so successful that it spawned five sequels: *After the Thin Man* (W. S. Van Dyke, 1936), *Another Thin Man* (W. S. Van Dyke, 1939), *Shadow of the Thin Man* (W. S. Van Dyke, 1941), *The Thin Man Goes Home* (Richard Thorpe, 1945), and *Song of the Thin Man* (Edward Buzzell, 1947). The format of these early films was lighter than the tone we now associate with the hard-boiled private eye. For example, *Murders in the Rue Morgue* features a mad scientist trying to turn women into apes, while the 1931 *Maltese Falcon* has a tone far less dark than John Houston's later adaptation in 1941 (Walton 176, 178). The darker tone that is more emblematic of what is considered to be noir emerged later with films such as *Double Indemnity* (Billy Wilder, 1944) and *The Postman Always Rings Twice* (Tay Garnett, 1946), both based on the books written by Cain. Still more movies originated from hard-boiled fiction. For instance, the film adaptation of Hammett's novel *The Glass Key* was released in 1942, directed by Stuart Heisler, while the movies *Murder, My Sweet* (Edward Dmytryk, 1944), *The Big Sleep* (Howard Hawks, 1946), *The Blue Dahlia* (George Marshall, 1946), and *Lady in the Lake* (Robert Montgomery, 1947) were all based on novels by Chandler.

This trend of hard-boiled detective novels ending up on movie screens was hardly accidental for two reasons. One, there was a definite and intentional synergy between crime writers and the entertainment industry. For instance, James M. Cain, author of *The Postman Always Rings Twice* (adapted into a movie seven different times) and *Double Indemnity* (adapted into a movie directed by Billy Wilder and released in 1944, featuring the work of Raymond Chandler on the screenplay) had been a scriptwriter for both Paramount and Columbia, although neither of those endeavors proved as successful as his later writing. Raymond Chandler was another famous fiction author who worked for Hollywood. In addition to his screenplay for *Double Indemnity*, Chandler also wrote the screenplay for Alfred Hitchcock's *Strangers on a Train*

(1951) and Irving Pichel's *And Now Tomorrow* (1944). Even Dashiell Hammett worked for Hollywood, writing the story for the 1931 film *City Streets* (directed by Rouben Mamoulian). This synergy was especially encouraged during the wartime years, when many Hollywood writers had been drafted, so the studios were starved for content. Second, as Mark Bould outlines in his book *Film Noir: From Berlin to Sin City*, less fiction was being published as a result of wartime rationing, contributing to the lack of available content, so prewar pulps seemed an obvious choice, a choice made even more obvious by the very language used in hard-boiled fiction (67). After all, most altercations were verbal, rather than reliant on expensive effects or complicated direction. During a time of budgetary constraints, talk could literally be cheap.

Many of these films featured the rough-around-the-edges private investigator or a suitable proxy, as in the case of *Double Indemnity*, the screenplay of which was cowritten by Raymond Chandler and Billy Wilder. A film noir classic that established the look and feel for many later films, *Double Indemnity* also influenced future detective narratives with its character of Barton Keyes (Edward G. Robinson), an insurance claims adjuster determined to expose Phyllis Dietrichson (Barbara Stanwyck) for murdering her husband and attempting to collect on the insurance claim.

Hard-boiled crime fiction also became integral to the early years of noir and gangster films. W. R. Burnett's crime novel *Little Caesar* became one of the first classic American gangster movies (directed by Mervyn Le Roy and released in 1931), and he also cowrote the gangster film *The Finger Points* (directed by John Francis Dillon and released in 1931), as well as providing the concept for *The Beast of the City* (directed by Charles Brabin and released in 1932), another classic gangster film. These films featured larger-than-life mobsters played by Humphrey Bogart, James Cagney, and Edward G. Robinson. In contrast to MGM and Paramount, studios with big stars and even bigger productions, Warner Bros. became known during the 1930s and '40s for these gangster movies. Specifically, the studio focused on "people living in cities, who are struggling, who are criminals," explains the film historian Saul Austerlitz. "If people went to see an MGM or Paramount film, it was because they wanted to be swept away. Warner Bros. was the diametric opposite of that" (qtd. in Wilkerson).

The popularity of these criminal narratives—with their dark atmosphere and depictions of gritty urban vitality—shaped the wave of hard-boiled detective narratives that followed, both on the screen and on the page. These narratives used crime to demonstrate the helplessness and frustration that many men felt following

World War II. Servicemen returning home found an America very different from the one they had left. Gender roles had changed, jobs were hard to find, and many returning servicemen were coping with physical injuries and/or emotional traumas suffered in combat. The American Dream started to feel like a lie.

FORMULA

Despite the many changes that took place in Los Angeles after the war, the template of the detective narrative, as laid out in Raymond Chandler's essay "Twelve Notes on the Mystery Story," remains strikingly apt today, demonstrating the persistent appeal of the L.A private eye in film, television, and literature. In that essay, Chandler outlines the various rules that any writer for a detective story should know. He argues that the detective story should feel credible, with the actions, the people, and the circumstances all appearing plausible. The author has an obligation not to mislead the reader, by either concealing relevant information or unfairly emphasizing facts that are not important. Chandler also felt that the story should be both simple enough to understand and complex enough to intrigue the intelligent reader. He cautioned against incorporating a love interest, arguing that that nearly always weakens a mystery story. The criminal and the detective must be different people, and, lastly, the criminal should be punished somehow, even if not by the legal system. Without this kind of resolution, there would be no satisfying closure for the reader ("Twelve Notes" 1004–1007).

To these rules, Chandler adds the argument that the most effective way to conceal a mystery is behind another mystery. The detective story must operate with two stories, one known to the criminal, detailing the crime and the attempts to conceal it, and one known to the author, which is the story told to the reader or viewer. Both stories must intermittently connect, with the hidden story appearing "here and there" (*Notebooks* 42). The reader or viewer must be distracted from figuring out the hidden story too quickly by being provided with "the wrong problem," which is "only tangential to the central problem" ("Casual Notes" 69). It is important for the audience to be distracted so that no one discovers the culprit before the detective does. While the audience is distracted by the surface story, the detective carefully steps back in time in order to put the events in their correct order so that he can reveal the hidden story properly.

And he always does so with a combination of analysis, deduction, and observation. Much as a certain comfort comes from believing in conspiracy theories—because it is better to think that someone is in control rather than face the scarier idea of a meaningless unknown—the detective story (temporarily) imposes order on chaos. There is comfort in the predictability that, no matter how complex, the detective will solve the case before the story ends. The detective cannot be bribed or distracted. His only purpose is to solve the case, and nothing can dissuade him from doing so.

The thrill of the detective narrative revolves around this discovery, around the reveal of information previously kept secret. Why do these detective stories (both in published and in cinematic form) remain so popular? The immediate response might be to argue that these narratives fulfill a deep-seated desire to see the bad punished and the good rewarded, but this is often a small percentage of the actual narrative. After all, the bad are not always necessarily punished. However, they are *discovered*. And it is this discovery that keeps us coming back for more.

In the successful detective story, there is a complicated relationship between the delay of the conclusion and the pleasure of the reader. Too little delay causes disappointment. Too much delay causes frustration. Dennis Porter, in his essay "Backward Construction and the Art of Suspense," argues that the mystery writer must strike a careful balance between "moving inexorably toward a conclusion" and "delaying the conclusion as long as possible to prolong the reader's pleasurable tension." It is this carefully modulated "suspense of the unanswered question" that fuels the detective story (327). The suspense of wondering who committed the crime in question is compounded by the suspense of wondering if the person will commit it again. The successful combination of these two questions fuels the narrative.

This suspense can be intensified as a result of several factors, such as the length of time between the initial events and the conclusion, the amount of sympathy for the characters involved, the intensity of the threat, and the desirability of the solution (Porter, "Backward Construction" 328, 329). Regardless of the external factors, it is the "braking of recognition" that becomes an essential component in the detective story (Shklovsky 66). The strategic delay of discovery can be fueled by distractions either by other characters or other subplots or by false solutions that impede progress toward the real solution, the inability to recognize clues for what they are, or the inability to distinguish between fake clues and real clues. But whatever the reason, every detective story will inevitably follow the same formula, and this is that formula:

1. The detective must figure out who committed the crime and why he or she did so. This crime must be important enough to make us (and the detective) care about its solution and complex enough to sustain our interest (and the detective's).

2. If the criminal is already known, then the detective must build enough evidence to prove the criminal's guilt. This option is much less common. Usually, if the criminal is known, it is discovered that the criminal (even if guilty of other crimes) is not guilty of the specific crime at hand.

3. There is at least one murder, and with the Los Angeles private eye, this murder is often tied to a much-larger case of corruption and conspiracy. It is seldom an isolated death.

4. Empathy is reserved for the potential next victim(s) in order to build suspense, but too much empathy will weigh the story down.

5. The first supposed solution is inevitably incorrect. Its failure usually sheds light on the actual solution.

6. Whatever happens to the criminal after apprehension is often irrelevant. The detective focuses on the discovery of the solution rather than the legal complications that follow.

7. Often the clues have been there all along, but it requires the unique perspective and intelligence of the detective to recognize them and thus provide the audience (viewer or reader) with the satisfying reveal.

Because detective narratives are so much about the construction of the narrative, about precise formulas that yield maximum audience enjoyment, they are rarely about the complex character of the detective himself. The character of the detective often stays the same—reassuringly so—in movie after movie, book after book, TV show after TV show. His name may change, but his characteristics remain constant. Similarly, the names of the femmes fatales, the villains, and the sidekicks may change, but their characteristics also remain constant. What the detective narrative does not offer with regard to character development, it makes up for in plot. Every detective narrative must reinvent the detective template enough not only to avoid repetition but also so that the criminal may elude discovery until most of the narrative has been told. The mechanics of the plot, the structure of the crime, must be somehow new and ingenious each time. After all, most readers and viewers of detective narratives tend to be aficionados of the genre, and while a certain amount of familiarity can be comforting, it is the responsibility of the writer to come up with a way to make each story feel different.

NEO-NOIR

One way to make the story different is through the lens of "neo-noir." In the book *Detours and Lost Highways: A Map of Neo-Noir*, Foster Hirsch writes that noir-like films, although they "appeared irregularly in the 1960s and 1970s," returned during the 1980s and 1990s, and it is these films that are frequently labeled as "neo-noir," with "neo" implying newness or reinvention. This revival of noir—otherwise described as the advent of neo-noir—was launched with films such as Paul Bogart's *Marlowe* in 1969, Robert Altman's *The Long Goodbye* in 1973, and John Huston's *Chinatown* in 1974, before going on to include such films as Ethan and Joel Coen's *Blood Simple* in 1984, Paul Verhoeven's *Basic Instinct* in 1991, John Dahl's *The Last Seduction* in 1994, and Curtis Hanson's *L.A. Confidential* in 1997.

While the detective's role remained much the same with regard to his occupation and methodology (in neo-noirs, he too struggles to expose criminals hidden behind wealth and/or power, traversing the expanse of Los Angeles in a rootless and restless way), the chief difference in this new version of the private eye is in his interactions with the surrounding world. He suffers even more under the weight of social alienation. The neo-noir private eye is lonely, ineffectual, trapped in "the grip of an existential crisis," and "lost in a world he cannot understand" (Nichol 45, 46, 47). This can be seen in Elliot Gould's portrayal of Philip Marlowe in Altman's *The Long Goodbye*, a portrayal that emphasizes Marlowe's "incompatibility with the modern world, . . . entirely unsuited to the real world" (Nichol 46), as well as in Gene Hackman's turn as private investigator Harry Moseby in *Night Moves* (Arthur Penn 1975), a character who refuses to take his wife's advice to join the modern world (opting instead to freelance as a private detective in an office with his name and "Confidential" on the door). Perhaps most memorable in the list of ineffectual neo-noir private eyes, however, is Jack Nicholson's portrayal of Jake Gittes in Roman Polanski's *Chinatown*.

Nowhere is the detective's world less reassuring or familiar than in *Chinatown*. Ironically, the success of the film is a result of just how differently the story is told from the original detective formula. Polanski deliberately leads our expectations astray, subverting our belief that the detective will succeed and that the femme fatale will villainize. Instead, the detective fails and the femme fatale becomes the victim. The world is too much for Gittes, and Gittes is not enough for Evelyn Mulwray.

Chinatown exemplifies the category of "neo-noir." One of the most obvious changes to the traditional noir formula is the use of color. Rather than using the blacks and whites common to the classic detective film, Polanski uses color strategically. While Polanski does have a full color palette at his disposal, he chooses a select range of colors for this film: yellow, brown, and orange. This limited color selection, along with a minimal use of blue, emphasizes the parched conditions in Los Angeles, providing a subtle but persistent reminder that the film revolves around a lack of water. Even the orange groves are shot to accentuate the dry and brown dirt taking up the bottom half of the frame. Some of the few sequences to feature lush green grass and water are the scenes shot at the house of the wealthy Noah Cross—and the water in his pool is salt water, so it still cannot help with thirst. This strategic use of color serves not only to convey the parched conditions of a dry Los Angeles but also to emphasizes the film's departure from tradition.

Like *Chinatown*, *L.A. Confidential* is filmed in color, setting it apart from the noir films that it clearly references, both thematically and stylistically. Also like *Chinatown*, director Curtis Hanson finds ways to reference the tones and atmosphere of traditional noir. For instance, many of the film's intense moments occur after dark or in dimly lit rooms. The lighting is rich and melodramatic, complete with frequent shadows even during the daytime scenes. Hanson uses the brilliant red of blood for a dramatic effect that was not available to previous directors, who were limited to blacks and whites. If anything, contemporary directors' use of color has created a new kind of film noir, one in which the conflict is not merely dark versus light but depicted with a range of colors, some muted, some vivid, but all used with the same intent: to highlight the darkness that lurks behind L.A.'s sunshine.

In a plot partly inspired by the California Water Wars and the Owens Valley conflict, Noah Cross (John Huston) in *Chinatown* plans to dry up the San Fernando Valley by diverting water away from it, buying the land once it becomes worthless, and then diverting the water back to the valley, making the land valuable again and leaving him with a huge profit. A woman claiming to be Evelyn Mulwray (daughter of Noah Cross) hires Jake Gittes to investigate her husband, Hollis Mulwray. As chief engineer for the Los Angeles Department of Water and Power, Hollis publicly opposes building a new reservoir because he knows that there is a conspiracy to divert the city's water supply in order to create the drought. Because of this, the fake Evelyn sets him up. Easily duped, Gittes photographs Hollis with a young woman, thinking that there is salacious intent, and the images are published in the local paper. It is only when the real Evelyn Mulwray (Faye Dunaway) turns up, furious with Gittes, that Gittes realizes he has been used. After Hollis Mulwray is murdered, the real Evelyn hires Gittes to investigate. At this point, as in *The Big Sleep*, the plot becomes inexorably complicated, having very little to do with the initial conspiracy that first set things in motion. Gittes and Evelyn discover Noah Cross's scam, become romantically involved, more people are murdered, rape and incest come into play, and the film ends with Cross seemingly untouchable and Gittes powerless. It is not just that Gittes is powerless but that his actions also lead directly to Evelyn's death. He does not merely fail. He makes the situation worse.

While much about Gittes demonstrates his shared lineage with figures such as Philip Marlowe and Sam Spade, much about him is also significantly different. One obvious difference relates to the year of release. Despite being set in 1937 Los Angeles, *Chinatown* was released in 1974, decades after the heyday of Marlowe and Spade. Those decades lent a perspective that only time could provide, allowing *Chinatown* to depict just how flawed and fractured the character of the L.A. private eye had become.

As was often the case with neo-noir, in *Chinatown*, Polanski plays specifically with our expectations for the genre in order to comment on it, to demonstrate its inadequacies. For instance, he rejected screenwriter Robert Towne's original ending, which he viewed as too traditional: "Towne wanted the evil tycoon to die and his daughter, Evelyn to live," explains Polanski. "I knew that if *Chinatown* was to be special, not just another thriller where the good guys triumph in the final reel, Evelyn had to die. Its dramatic impact would be lost unless audiences left their seats with a sense of outrage" (348). And so, at the end of the film, instead of a successful showdown between Jake and Evelyn's father, Noah Cross, Gittes is disarmed, Evelyn is shot, and the only evidence linking the murderer to the scene of the crime is removed. In the article "'The Injustice of It All': Polanski's Revision of the Private Eye Genre in *Chinatown*," James Maxfield writes, "The film ends with the villain triumphant, the hero defeated, and the heroine dead—the expected ending of a detective film turning completely upside down" (93). It is true that hard-boiled private eye narratives rarely have joyous resolutions, but there is usually some attempt at punishment for the wrongdoers, regardless of whether that punishment is officially sanctioned. In *Chinatown*, the ending is bitter without any sweet.

However, the ending is not the only place where expectations are manipulated. Despite Evelyn Mulwray's superficial resemblance to classic femme fatales, Polanski plays on our expectations for her, to show us both that our assumptions are incorrect and that Gittes is wrong too. Gittes, in many ways, is an atypical private eye, especially when compared to the mold established by Philip Marlowe in *The Big Sleep*. Not only is he wrong about Evelyn, but he does not have the self-restraint and integrity we have grown to expect from our private eyes. Unlike Marlowe, he is slow to pick up on the clues surrounding him. Although women intentionally mislead both Gittes and Marlowe, Gittes takes much longer to realize the subterfuge, actually falling for the ruse perpetuated by the false Evelyn Mulwray and playing right into her scheme. He does not realize his error until the real Evelyn is standing in front of him.

This is not the only time Gittes is wrong; his sleuthing instincts prove more fallible than most. The large bandage across Gittes's nose during the second half of the film further emphasizes his lack of prowess, not only a demonstration of his failures as a detective and as a man but also a punishment for his "nosiness." Much as *Chinatown* depicts Los Angeles as the illusion of a magical paradise—corruption, rape, incest, murder lurking behind the scenes—Gittes offers only the illusion of the hard-boiled private eye. Gittes may imitate the appearance of the traditional private eye, but this performance remains just a poor imitation. The end of the film serves to emphasize his failures, both personal and professional. Interestingly, screenwriter Robert Towne had initially envisioned Gittes as "a glamorous, successful operator, a snappy dresser with a coolly insolent manner—a new archetypal detective figure," but Polanski disagreed, determined to portray Gittes as "no pale, down-at-heel imitation of Marlowe" (Polanski 303). By doing so, as well as by significantly changing the film's ending, Polanski depicts the fundamental flaws at the heart of the L.A. private eye.

The wave of hard-boiled detective films that propelled their way through the 1970s—such as *The Long Goodbye* (Robert Altman, 1973), *Chinatown* (Roman Polanski, 1974), *Farewell, My Lovely* (Dick Richards, 1975), *Night Moves* (Arthur Penn 1975), and the second adaptation of *The Big Sleep* (Michael Winner, 1978)—seem most concerned, despite their emphasis on political and social corruption, with just how ineffectual the hard-boiled detective had become, how out of place in a modern world. In *The Long Goodbye*, for instance, Philip Marlowe, as played by Elliot Gould, could not be more different from the Marlowe established by Humphrey Bogart several decades earlier. Whereas Bogart's Marlowe looked and felt utterly at home on the "mean streets" of Los Angeles, Gould's Marlowe seems totally out of place with his vintage car and vintage suits. As Bran Nichol writes, Gould's Marlowe is incompatible with the world around him, "oddly domesticated" and standing for "values which are now defunct," while Robert Mitchum's Marlowe, in *Farewell, My Lovely*, suggests "that the species of detective he represents is on the point of extinction" (46, 47, 128). The director Arthur Penn explains that what interested him about the character of Harry Moseby "was being able to show a man who, without being a true outsider, is nevertheless alienated from the society in which he lives. He's unable to establish meaningful connections with the world and other people" (qtd. in Coursodon 112). These private eyes, much like Gittes, are hopelessly adrift.

However, while Polanski may have thought he was exposing the cracks at the heart of the L.A. private eye and the detective genre as a whole, he was more in line with Chandler than he realized. Chandler wrote in a letter to his agent regarding the novel *The Long Goodbye* (published in 1953), "I didn't care *whether the mystery was fairly obvious*, but I cared about the people, about the strange corrupt world we live in, and how any man who tried to be honest looks in the end either sentimental or plain foolish" ("Chandler on His Novels" 233; emphasis in original).

There is no question that *Chinatown* is a depiction of the "strange corrupt world we live in" and that Gittes, by trying to be honest, sets himself up for defeat. To say he looks foolish may be an understatement. The bandage on his nose and the dead body of Evelyn Mulwray serve as glaring reminders of his failures. Tellingly, Gittes used to work for the district attorney in Chinatown, and he tells Evelyn that when he was there, he did "as little as possible." It is precisely Gittes's choice *not* to do as little as possible, to try instead to rectify wrongs and save the girl, that leads to his failure and her death. The implicit message is that if he had just kept doing as little as possible, things would actually have turned out better.

TELEVISION

Much like the private eye on film, the private eye on television similarly works and lives alone. With a description that is equally as apt for the private eye in film or literature, Mareike Jenner writes that the TV detective is "a maverick outsider who is frequently defined through eccentric behavior and a superior mental ability (often in stark contrast to the inevitably slow-witted policeman he reluctantly has to deal with)" (20). Jenner references the character of Adrian Monk (Tony Shaloub) from the television show *Monk* (USA, 2002–2009), using him as an example of characters with a disability or personality disorder—in the case of Monk, obsessive compulsive disorder—which limits their social interactions but which also serves "to enhance their abilities as detectives, making connections or observing minute details others overlook" (20). Jenner notes that this enhanced ability allows the detective not only to uncover "the truth about a particular case" but also to uncover the truth about society at large, a characteristic shared with other detectives (21). It is precisely the outsider's perspective that enables the detective to make his astute observations.

Early examples of the L.A. private eye on television include *Peter Gunn* (NBC, 1958–1960; ABC, 1960–1961), *Mannix* (CBS, 1967–1975), *The Rockford Files* (NBC,

1974–1980), *Matt Houston* (ABC, 1982–1985), and *Riptide* (NBC, 1984–1986). All these shows were unapologetically action driven, taking the clever verbal repartee of earlier private eyes and replacing it with infinite car chases and hyperbolic theme music. Physical strength and endurance were now an essential component of the job, along with a well-chiseled body.

Created by Blake Edwards, best remembered as the creator of the Pink Panther films, *Peter Gunn* stars Craig Stevens as the sophisticated private eye behind the wheel of a Plymouth Fury convertible. Released in 1967, a feature film version, titled *Gunn*, was directed by Edwards and also starred Stevens in the title role. The inspiration for the character came from a radio series, also created by Edwards, titled *Richard Diamond, Private Detective* that aired from 1949 to 1953 and that was brought to television starring David Janssen (CBS, 1957–1959; NBC, 1959–1960). The first two seasons of *Richard Diamond, Private Detective* were set in New York City, and later seasons took place in Los Angeles. The opening credits—featuring high-contrast black and white, along with the figure of Janssen silhouetted, wearing a hat, and smoking—evoke the classic film noir aesthetic. Diamond also drove a convertible, in his case, first a 1959 DeSoto Fireflite and then a 1959 Ford Galaxie. The predisposition of the private eye toward driving a convertible continues through the present day, although it was a predisposition limited to a select type of private eye, one that needed to be watched as he or she was doing the watching.

Joe Mannix (Mike Connors), the title character of *Mannix*, originally worked for Intertect, a large, technology-based detective agency in Los Angeles. However, as befits the rogue private eye, Mannix does not like to follow the rules, does not trust computers, and prefers to take matters into his own hands, literally. Eventually, he leaves Intertect to form his own agency. The opening sequence for the show features Mannix in a range of Bond-like scenarios, racing around town in his various cars, evading capture, getting into fistfights, tumbling down a cliff, and kissing an enthusiastic blond bombshell. He, like Diamond, drives convertibles, including a 1966 Mercury Comet Caliente, a 1967 Mercury Comet Cyclone, a 1968 Dodge Dart, a 1969 Dodge Dart, a 1970 Plymouth Cuda, and a 1973 Plymouth Cuda.

The Rockford Files was cocreated by Roy Huggins, who had also created the television show *Maverick* (ABC, 1957–1962), which, along with shows such as *Cheyenne* (ABC, 1955–1963), *Colt .45* (ABC, 1957–1960), and *Bronco* (ABC, 1958–1962), made up the Warner Bros. roster of westerns. Huggins himself describes *The Rockford Files* as a modern-day *Maverick*. Both Maverick and Rockford—the lead characters of the two shows—are loners, with Rockford an outsider because of his background as an ex-con and Maverick an outsider by choice. Clearly, Huggins felt that the best way to modernize a western hero was to make him a private detective, thus reinforcing the notion of the private eye as the natural successor to the cowboy.

A wrongfully sentenced ex-con, Rockford focuses on "cold cases," also known as cases that the Los Angeles Police Department cannot solve. He intentionally does not pursue cases that are under open investigation so as to avoid stepping on anyone's toes, a sense of decorum unusual for a private eye. Huggins created the show with Stephen J. Cannell, who was determined to reinvent the detective genre by making private detective Jim Rockford (James Garner) an atypical private eye. Rockford's cynical approach is emphasized by the occasional appearance of Tom Selleck as Lance White, a fellow private eye who, in contrast, exudes a little too much optimism, sincerity, and integrity. For instance, in the episode "White on White and Nearly Perfect," the "nearly perfect" White turns down a potential client who had initially hired Rockford, explaining that "ethics are ethics" and "they don't change when the price goes up" (NBC, October 20, 1978). Integrity, however, is not always Rockford's leading motivator. Nonetheless, he still rarely makes money as many of his clients avoid paying their fees.

Produced by Aaron Spelling, *Matt Houston* stars Lee Horsley as the eponymous son of a Texas oilman, sent to California to supervise his family's offshore drilling enterprise. In his spare time, Houston becomes a private investigator. The show is an over-the-top mix of mustachioed Houston racing from one dramatic scenario to the next, with an emphasis on car chases, explosions, scantily clad women, and sometimes even a scantily clad Houston. Matt Houston, too, was predisposed to the convertible. Much like Huggins and Cannell, Spelling wanted to update or reinvent the template of the private detective narrative, and he did so by amping up the action and adventure, in a style even more sensationalized than *Mannix*.

Scantily clad women are all over *Riptide*, a show that gives the tropes of the private detective a twist in that the Pier 56 Detective Agency (later known as the Riptide Detective Agency) is run by *two* detectives—Cody Allen (Perry King) and Nick Ryder (Joe Penny), who served in Vietnam together—along with a computer hacker to serve their technological needs. Unusually, the agency operates from a boat, the *Riptide*. Fittingly, chase sequences are not limited to cars but also incorporate boats and even helicopters. Eventually scheduled against *Moonlighting* in 1986, the show's cancellation became imminent, and so the writers cleverly wrote a penultimate episode in which Allen, Ryder, and their hacker give up detecting in favor of consulting for Hollywood.

Regardless of the countless variations to the detective story over the years—the ebb and flow of action and spectacle, the ever-evolving shape of the convertible, the adroitness with which the detective navigates his world, the proximity to babes in bikinis, the nuance and importance of language—one constant rings true: the private eye is a straight, white male.

3

THE DETECTIVE

But down these mean streets a man must go who is not himself mean, who is neither tarnished nor afraid. The detective in this kind of story must be such a man. He is the hero, he is everything. He must be a complete man and a common man and yet an unusual man. He must be, to use a rather weathered phrase, a man of honor, by instinct, by inevitability, without thought of it, and certainly without saying it. He must be the best man in his world and a good enough man for any world. . . . If there were enough like him, I think the world would be a very safe place to live in, and yet not too dull to be worth living in.

—Raymond Chandler, "The Simple Art of Murder"

WHITE KNIGHT IN A COOL CADILLAC

Various conditions led to the rise of the hard-boiled private detective during the 1920s and 1930s. Distrust of government institutions encouraged the rise of the outsider who trusted no one. Frustration with corporations and big business made being self-employed all the more appealing. Growing fears of crime romanticized the figure of a man who was not afraid of anyone or anything, while a general feeling of suffocation within the domestic enclave made the eternal loner a figure of fascination. As Dennis Porter writes in his book *The Pursuit of Crime: Art and Ideology in Detective Fiction*, the private detective appeals as a folk hero, seen as free "in a world where the great majority recognize themselves to be under some form of bondage" (180). The private detective is both an inspiration—a reminder that such things are possible—and a salve for those who yearn to be free.

In the decades since Philip Marlowe first emerged as a celluloid icon, the figure of the L.A. private eye continues to appeal as he (and it is almost always a "he") investigates crimes on both large and small screens. In a world that seems to lack reason and morality, there is comfort in the consistent logic and integrity of our detective. We observe human nature through his detached perspective, and it somehow makes sense. We respect his devotion to the case and his corresponding disinterest in money. He is the Lone Ranger in a Cadillac or Lincoln. A hero who reports to no one, he is his own boss, a loner with no obligation other than to the truth. He may not be educated and may even have a healthy skepticism about so-called experts and their affiliated institutions; but he has street smarts, and those always prove more useful in the end. He operates via his own code, a deeply personal determination of right versus wrong. Unlike a police officer, whose actions are constricted by rules and regulations, the private eye only has his own code to follow, and his integrity rests on how well this code is followed. In Chandler's novel *The Long Goodbye*, Marlowe describes himself as a romantic. Unlike other people, who shut their windows and turn up the TV when they hear someone crying, Marlowe goes to see what happened, even if he realizes, "You don't make a dime that way. You got sense. . . . Stay out of other people's troubles. All it can get you is the smear" (229). But Marlowe has something stronger than "sense." He has his code.

In the book *Private Eyes: One Hundred and One Knights*, Robert A. Baker and Michael T. Nietzel describe this code of conduct as a descendant of the one followed by knights in medieval Europe: "Medieval knights pledged to protect the weak and oppressed—the poor, the widow, and the orphan. . . . Like their chivalrous predecessors, our modern knights are loved by us because at times it seems they are the only defenders of truth, justice, and morality in a world of deceit, senseless cruelty and immorality where life is never fair and nice guys finish last" (7). Chandler makes the metaphor literal in his novel *The Big Sleep* when Marlowe notices a stained-glass panel over the entrance doors to General Sternwood's mansion. This panel depicts a knight in armor rescuing a lady tied to a tree. Marlowe observes that the knight is "fiddling with the knots on the ropes that tied the lady to the tree" (Chandler, *Big Sleep* 3). Noticing the knight's apparent lack of success, Marlowe thinks to himself that the knight might need help, and so is born "the private eye as knight figure, as rescuer of the weak and defenseless" (Margolies 71–72).

Both traditional and hard-boiled detective narratives can be defined through the character of the detective at their center. While the traditional detective narrative relies on a detective whose keen insight and powers of deduction enable him to solve crimes, even while miles away from the actual crime scene, the hard-boiled detective must utilize physicality to traverse the urban landscape in search of clues, witnesses, and the truth. This physicality is also reminiscent of the knight imagery, as knights are compelled to traverse the landscape in pursuit of truth and justice. As Fredric Jameson describes in his book *Raymond Chandler: Detections of Totality*, the "detective no longer inhabits the atmosphere of pure thought, of puzzle-solving, and the resolution of a set of given elements. On the contrary, he is propelled outwards into the space of his world and obliged to move from one kind of social reality to another" (24). The code cannot be upheld from the comforts of the home or an office. The code can only be upheld by physical action and pursuit. The good must be rescued and the bad must be captured, and in order to do so, the private detective penetrates physical façades that might keep others out. He also penetrates mental façades, discovering secrets that might be hidden from everyone else. All while taking us with him on his journey.

Unlike Hercule Poirot, who could almost always solve a crime by exercising his "little grey cells," or Sherlock Holmes, who could solve a crime by thinking about it enough, the Los Angeles detective is rarely at home or at his office, much less sitting still. The L.A. private eye cannot solve cases in a vacuum. Instead, he must traverse the expanse of Los Angeles county in order to collect the right information, speak with the right people, and initiate the right results. Only he can drag the criminal rich out of the safety and exclusivity of the hills, back down to the flatland, "back to their histories, their crimes," demonstrating the inescapabilty of their transgressions and the inability of their wealth to protect them from him (Fine 125). Literally and metaphorically, the male private eye demonstrates a facility with the conquest of space. It is not only that the detective can traverse the physical terrain of Los Angeles but also that he can take people with him.

In the "Lincoln Lawyer" series of books, author Michael Connelly does away with an office altogether.

The character Mickey Haller, realizing that he is never in his actual office, converts his car into an office, hence the name "Lincoln Lawyer" for his choice of mobile office. Driven by former clients working off their debts to him, Haller conducts meetings and phone calls from the back seat of his car as he moves between destinations, rarely sedentary. Similarly, in the television show *The Rockford Files* (NBC, 1974–1980), James Garner lives and works in a mobile home parked somewhere in Malibu. In the episode "Backlash of the Hunter Part 1" (NBC, March 24, 1974), a potential client asks, surprised, if this trailer is also his office. Rockford replies, "Yeah, it's cheap, tax deductible, earthquake-proof.... I get a job out of town, I take it with me."

In many traditional detective stories, as with Agatha Christie's Poirot (who had Captain Hastings) or Arthur Conan Doyle's Holmes (who had Doctor Watson), the detective frequently has a sidekick. In contrast, the hard-boiled detective mainly works alone, adding to his rootlessness. In order to solve crimes, he has no one to rely on other than himself, which may partially explain why he so frequently is cynical, jaded, and/or irritable. If he does have a sidekick, it is more in the role of an assistant or a secretary. In the episode "Mr. Monk Goes to the Office" (USA, July 29, 2005), Monk (Tony Shaloub) literally goes undercover at an office. Much to his delight, he discovers the wonders of office camaraderie. "I could never be a detective," he tells his newfound friends. "They're lonely. They're—they're very lonely . . . and sad. They don't have a gang. A gang from the office." Unfortunately, Monk's camaraderie is short-lived, and soon it is back to his lonely life. The detective's loner status is an integral component of his personality. He cannot be seen as too attached to children, family, significant others, or colleagues. It is precisely his stance as an outsider that provides him with the unique perspective that enables his effective observations, as well as keeps him objective and clear-headed. In this way, too, the detective is the modern-day cowboy, riding into town as needed, keeping everyone at arm's length, and always just a bit cooler than anyone around him.

COWBOYS

The *Lincoln Lawyer* film, directed by Brad Furman and released in 2011, is not only an adaptation of the book of the same name by Michael Connelly but a fascinating example of the current relevance of the private eye archetype. As a contemporary incarnation of the classic Phillip Marlowe character, Mickey Haller (played by Matthew McConaughey) seems equally in control with the family of his wealthy client as with the local biker club, too rough around the edges to play by all the rules but not so rough as to disregard his own personal code or to look too out of place. As befits the tropes of the private eye, Haller has a complicated relationship with his ex-wife (played by Marisa Tomei) and daughter (played by Mackenzie Aladjem). He loves them both but seems incapable of having a functional relationship with either. Lorna Taylor (Pell James), Haller's secretary and case manager, is also his second ex-wife. While Haller operates out of his car, Lorna operates out her apartment, which occasionally doubles as a physical meeting place for Haller and his associates. Haller has an additional associate in the character of Frank Levin (William H. Macy), who assists in procuring photos and evidence. When Levin is killed during the film, Haller must investigate that murder as well.

Haller, as a modern-day cowboy, rides his Lincoln like a horse through the mean streets of Los Angeles. This analogy not only serves to combine images of both the old West (full of saloons, horses, and outlaws) and the new West (full of studios, cars, and actors) but also helps to explain the character of the private eye and, specifically, his masculinity. In the book *Which Way Did He Go? The Private Eye in Dashiell Hammett, Raymond Chandler, Chester Himes, and Ross Macdonald*, Edward Margolies argues in favor of the comparison between the detective and the cowboy: "With fewer and fewer animals to hunt and rustlers and Indians to shoot, the western hero turned to the city to pursue other prey. No longer a lone ranger of sorts, he became a private eye—still outside organized society, but curiously trapped inside as well" (6).

Here, again, we see the significance of Los Angeles as the private eye's terrain. John Irwin emphasizes that the private detective represents the "desire for personal freedom" that "has been central to American identity from the outset" (36) and that can be reflected by the private eye's move from "salaried employee of a large private agency or of the DA's office to being a self-employed, independent contractor" (77), as seen, for instance, in the stories of Raymond Chandler and Dashiell Hammett or in the television show *Mannix*. The private eye echoes the cowboys from those Wild West frontier towns, only he must contend with city streets and city crime.

The analogy of the detective as cowboy also helps to explain the problematic representations of women within the genre. Margolies links the hard-boiled detective's ambivalence toward women to that of the frontiersman, who identified women "with organized social institutions such as family, church, the schools, and the arts" (6). As a result of their affiliation with these institutions, women threatened to imprison men "in a tainted polity and dampen their idealism with the pragmatic demands of a domestic life" (6). Frontiersman averse to such imprisonment had no choice but to flee. Similarly, the hard-boiled detective must avoid affiliation with institutions such as family or the church. If the private eye is foolish enough to get married, the marriage cannot last, and a complicated relationship with the ex—or multiple exes—is guaranteed, which is exactly what plays out in *Lincoln Lawyer*.

The element of the West as the private eye's terrain serves another purpose. It sets up an effective contrast with the East Coast and the established figures common to it. As Dennis Porter writes, the East Coast is home to "American political power, its social elite, and most prestigious institutions of higher learning," a marked difference from the private eye, who is often "without a college education as well as lower class" (*Pursuit*, 175). The hard-boiled detective is a man of simple tastes and modest salary. His vices are often smoking and/or alcohol. He is at least somewhat self-destructive. Anything highly technological is usually beyond him, but he always knows someone who can help, by enhancing surveillance footage or hacking into email or tapping someone's phone. If he uses a computer at all, it is usually only to access records from the Department of Motor Vehicles or to search for a name or an address. This is not a character that feels at home in prestigious institutions or among the social elite.

THE POLICE DETECTIVE

While the police detective is rarely portrayed on television or in films as being a part of prestigious institutions or a member of the social elite, the police detective's affiliation with his or her own police department, as well as other police departments, and, in turn, the Federal Bureau of Investigation, embeds the police detective within a large network of government institutions. The private detective, on the other hand, is affiliated with neither networks nor institutions.

The police procedural became popular on television largely as a result of the success of *Dragnet*, which was first a successful radio show from 1949 to 1951, then a successful television show on the NBC television network from 1952 to 1959, and then again with a revival TV show from 1967 to 1970, all three incarnations featuring Jack Webb as actor and producer. There were also film versions in 1954, 1966, and 1987. The success of *Dragnet* led to the creation of countless other televised police procedurals, including *Starsky and Hutch* (ABC, 1975–1979, and a film adaptation directed by Todd Philips and released in 2004), *Cagney & Lacey* (CBS, 1981–1988), *Miami Vice* (NBC, 1984–1990, and a film adaptation directed by Michael Mann and released in 2006), *Law & Order* (NBC, 1990–2010), *Homicide: Life on the Street* (NBC, 1993–1999), and *NYPD*

Blue (ABC, 1993–2005). The police procedural offers two distinct differences from the hard-boiled private eye: an emphasis on institutionally enforced rules and regulations (unlike the private eye, who bends rules to suit his purpose) and a reliance on teamwork to get the job done (unlike the private eye, who almost always solves cases on his own).

As every rule requires an exception, so too does this one. The television show *The Shield* toys with our expectations of the distinct differences between police detectives and private eyes. Airing on the FX network from 2002 to 2008, the American crime drama reinvented not only the police procedural but also depictions of police activity on television, by subverting the traditional police/private investigator binary. Revolving around the adventures of detective Vic Mackey (Michael Chiklis) and the cops under his command in the fictional Farmington area of Los Angeles, the show exposes the corrupt behavior of an elite police division known as the Strike Team.

Unlike traditional police procedurals, *The Shield* drags story lines through multiple episodes (and possibly never wraps them up). Rather than depict the typical police detective, who respects rules and regulations, as well as the basic code of human behavior, Mackey and his cohorts often rely on illegal and abusive behavior in order to solve their cases and pad their own "retirement funds." On the one hand, Mackey has much more in common with the hard-boiled private eye than with a standard police detective (going above and beyond in order to protect those who need protecting, for instance), but on the other hand, his propensity for violence and his disregard for the ethics of the law (threatening to plant drugs on a potential informant if he does not cough up the information Mackey wants, killing a cop who might expose Mackey's corruption, humiliating a fellow cop who makes the mistake of taking Mackey's ex-wife out on a date) sets Mackey up in a different category entirely. The relationship between him and his more law-abiding colleagues is antagonistic, to say the least. Mackey becomes a true antihero, a man whose tactics make you cringe but whose final motivations are uncomfortably agreeable, even if the repeated message is that whatever good comes out of Mackey's behavior will often be overshadowed by the bad.

In marked contrast is Shane Vendrell (Walton Goggins), a member of Mackey's Strike Team who during season 4 heads off to the vice squad, where he seems determined to make himself over in Mackey's image. Unfortunately, he lacks Mackey's moral center, and Shane's primary motivations appear to be power and profit. While Mackey is the ultimate rogue cop who makes up his own rules but still follows his own code of conduct (women and children are always protected, for instance), Shane depicts the ultimate corrupt cop who has no regard for the badge beyond its ability to benefit him directly.

During the late 1990s, the Los Angeles Police Department (LAPD) was rocked by a scandal credited with directly inspiring *The Shield*. An investigation into LAPD's Rampart Division resulted in accusations of corruption targeted at the division's antigang unit. Not only was Officer Rafael Perez accused of stealing at least six pounds of cocaine from the LAPD property room, but there were also claims of unprovoked shootings (including the March 1997 killing of the black off-duty LAPD Officer Kevin Gaines by the white LAPD Officer Frank Lyga), a November 1997 bank robbery masterminded by LAPD Officer David Mack, abuse of suspects (such as the February 1998 beating of the handcuffed gang member Ismael Jimenez by LAPD Officer Brian Hewitt or the October 1996 shooting and framing of nineteen-year-old Javier Francisco Ovando by Perez and Officer Nino Duren that left Ovando paralyzed from the waist down), and numerous wrongful arrests, leading to overturned convictions, including Ovando's. Much like with the work of Dashiell Hammett and James Cain, Shawn Ryan, creator of *The Shield*, knows that the best crime stories borrow from reality. Unlike the cozy mystery, the hard-boiled detective tale—and in this case, the unconventional police drama—brings the mystery to the streets, where it serves as social commentary, a reflection of real urban life rather than reassuring fantasy.

John Sumser argues in his study of morality and social order in television crime dramas that it is precisely the subjugation of a cop's individual authority to the letter of the law that serves as a kind of moral handicap; a clear sense of justice and moral certainty is sacrificed when bureaucratized law enforcement requires not only that a crime be solved but also that it be solved in a way that permits successful prosecution (154, 155). While there have been some depictions of successful detectives within official police departments—such as George Simenon's Inspector Maigret, F. W. Croft's Inspector French, Michael Connelly's Hieronymous Bosch, or any of the regular cast of *Law & Order: Special Victims Unit* (NBC, 1999–present)—fans of the detective genre know that these exceptions make up only 10 to 20 percent of portrayals of fictional police officer, writes Richard Alewyn. Even when police detectives are hardworking and ambitious, they are most often portrayed as "nothing more than capable routinists, . . . narrow-minded and unimaginative" (Alewyn 67). Unless, of course, they are Vic Mackey. In the case of Mackey, it is precisely the qualities that he shares with the hard-boiled private investigator that set him apart from those capable routinists.

Contrasting the police department with the private eye highlights the strengths, difficulties, and responsibilities that come with being the "rogue player." While the police department has access to "an unlimited apparatus of persons and resources," in these narratives, it is the independent detective—without colleagues, state institution, wife, or children—who most often discovers the truth (Alewyn 67). It is the outsider, with one foot in the underworld and one foot in respectable society, who protects the innocent and punishes the guilty. The implication is that it is precisely the private detective's status as outsider, as eccentric or bohemian—as opposed to civil servant or even ordinary civilian—that explains his success (Alewyn 68). The same applies to Mackey, whose familiarity with drug dealers, prostitutes, and gang leaders is directly responsible for his high case-closure rate. As Mackey himself puts it, in the pilot episode of *The Shield* (FX, March 12, 2002), "Good cop and bad cop have left for the day. . . . I'm a different kind of cop," before beginning to beat a suspect with a phone book. Mackey, like the private eye, also has the advantage of being able to traverse the underworld in a way unavailable to law-abiding members of the police force. However, the ability to think like a criminal and see the world like a criminal sets both Mackey and the private eye apart from "'good' society and the benefits of that society, including community, marriage, and family"; instead, the private detective must remain, like the frontiersman, "a lone hero" (Gates 85). And this is why the failure of Mackey's marriage should come as no surprise to fans of the genre.

A LONE HERO

One of the interesting qualities of Curtis Hanson's 1997 neo-noir *L.A. Confidential* is the way it similarly incorporates elements of the traditional private eye and the corrupt cop with the trope of the law-abiding policeman into the characters of three different members of the Los Angeles Police Department. Despite being members of a police force and, in turn, a bureaucratic network, the three policemen at the heart of the film are all fundamental loners at heart. The film is set in 1953, and Ed Exley (Guy Pearce) uses police corruption as leverage to get himself promoted to detective lieutenant. His adherence to rules and regulations, combined with his disregard for policeman loyalty, earns him no points with his fellow officers and sets him up as a pariah. The two other protagonists are Officer Bud White (Russell Crowe), who combines a temper with an intense obligation to protect women, and Sergeant Jack Vincennes (Kevin Spacey), a narcotics detective who shamelessly exploits his arrests in order to get himself more publicity. These three men, all with very different agendas, independently discover massive corruption within the police department.

As Officer Dick Stensland (Graham Beckel) arrives at the police station's Christmas party, alcohol in tow, a fellow police officer asks why he is late. Stensland explains that his partner, Officer White, had to stop "to help a damsel in distress. He's got his priorities all screwed up." The fellow officer laughs. We instantly know what kind of police department this is—as if real-life events had not already told us—and we also know of White's awkward fit within it. When Ed Exley is asked why he became a cop, his answer—"I like to help people"—seems charmingly naïve. The awkward fit of both Exley and White, much like the awkward fit of Mackey within his own department, provides us with characters who—for better and for worse—are not part of their own institution, following their own code rather than the sanctioned rules of their own specific departments, managing to balance elements of the hard-boiled private eye within an increasingly untrustworthy police department.

When Vincennes approaches Captain Dudley Smith (James Cromwell), not realizing Smith's own involvement with the corruption, Smith kills Vincennes. Smith also deliberately manipulates White, hoping to persuade him to kill Exley out of jealousy, but Exley instead convinces White of Smith's guilt. Exley and White begin to work together to gather evidence to convict Smith of setting up a heroin-distribution empire in Los Angeles. Smith, knowing that Exley and White are on to him, sets them up, but they manage to survive, killing Smith in the process. As befits a hard-boiled narrative, not only are the various story lines complex and interconnected— weaving together police corruption with prostitution, drugs, and organized crime—but the final resolution is also uneasy, as the LAPD covers up the corruption in order to protect its reputation, concealing any of Smith's wrongdoing. As James Ellroy, author of the original book on which the film was based, explains, "I've long held that hard-boiled crime fiction is the history of bad white men doing bad things in the name of authority" (qtd. in Sragow).

L.A. Confidential was released on September 19, 1997, almost exactly two years after O. J. Simpson's acquittal and right before the Rampart Division scandal exploded. The film felt anchored in history and social context. To anchor its portrayal of police corruption, the film also repurposed actual historical events such as Bloody Christmas, when as many as fifty LAPD officers attending a departmental Christmas party pulled six prisoners out of the Central City Jail and beat them for over ninety minutes. Once again, real-life events enabled the fictional narrative to double as social commentary. Unlike real life, however, in which the LAPD kept the event out of the media for several months, the outrage in *L.A. Confidential* is almost immediate. Hanson knew that his audience could only stomach so much corruption and cruelty.

4

THE BLACK DETECTIVE

And if people respect Easy, I think it's not because of his
hard past, but because he has taken on a tough job in the
real world: he's trying to define himself in spite of the
world, to live by his own system of values. He's trying
to do what is right in an imperfect world. The genre may
be mystery, but the underlying questions are moral and
ethical, even existential.

—Walter Mosley, "The Black Dick"

HISTORY

The first film with a black detective as the protagonist
was *A Black Sherlock Holmes*, directed by R. J. Philips and
released in 1918. Running for a total of twelve minutes, the
film featured an all-black cast and starred Sam Robinson
as detective Knick Carter and Rudolph Tatum as his assistant, Reuma Tism. Not only a parody of the original Sherlock Holmes character, *A Black Sherlock Holmes* is also
an example of the "race films" popular in the early part of

the twentieth century and targeted at African American audiences. While the companies producing these films were usually white owned, the casts were African American, and the content of the films was designed to appeal to audiences disgusted by D. W. Griffith's *Birth of a Nation* (1915), as well as by the otherwise-demeaning portrayals of blacks in standard Hollywood fare.

Unfortunately, *A Black Sherlock Holmes* failed with black audiences, who found the caricature performances humiliating. The production company behind the film— Ebony Film Corporation—found many of its releases similarly ignored by African American audiences. The newspaper the *Chicago Defender*, which had primarily African American readers, criticized the company's releases, saying that they caused "respectable ladies and gentlemen to blush with shame and humiliation" (Sampson 207). The company went out of business a few years later. Ironically, however, *A Black Sherlock Holmes* was a success with white audiences, who enjoyed the "original and inborn sense of humor," according to a review in the *Exhibition Herald* (Sampson 241).

Perhaps because of the film's commercial and critical failure among its target audience, or perhaps because of generalized racism in the United States, Knick Carter was the only black detective protagonist to appear onscreen until the release of *In the Heat of the Night* (Norman

Jewison, 1967), almost fifty years later. In that film, Sidney Poitier plays Virgil Tibbs, a black police detective from Philadelphia—although he hails from California in the original book—sent to Sparta, Mississippi, to assist in the investigation of the murder of a wealthy industrialist. Despite that film's success, films about African American detectives continue to remain few and far between.

SIDEKICKS AND SUPPORTING ACTORS

Even though the detective narrative is primarily about the triumph of good over injustice and evil, that triumph almost exclusively happens at the hands of white men. As Philippa Gates writes, in her book *Detecting Men: Masculinity and the Hollywood Detective Film*, when "otherness" does show up in the detective genre, usually in the form of racial or ethnic difference, it is often reserved for the role of the villain or the sidekick, not someone at the center of the narrative. This way, the racial or ethnic (or even sexual) other functions as an effective contrast from "the heroism and Americanness of the protagonist," defined or enhanced by his whiteness and masculinity (Gates 95). For instance, a survey of the television show *COPS*—a reality show that follows police officers on the job, airing on FOX from 1989 and 2013 before moving to Spike (now known as the Paramount Network)—found that the vast majority of police officers shown were white males (92 percent) and that the majority of offenders were nonwhite (62 percent). These numbers are completely skewed, making African Americans seem much more likely to be guilty and making white males appear less guilty than in real life (Monk-Turner et al.). Similar ratios are reflected on fictional shows, where there is usually one token African American member of the police force—*CSI: Crime Scene Investigation* (CBS, 2000–2015), *Criminal Minds* (CBS, 2005–present), *Southland* (NBC, 2009; TNT, 2010–2013), and *Law & Order: Special Victims Unit* (NBC, 1999–present) are four examples.

The *Beverly Hills Cop* film franchise, starring Eddie Murphy as Axel Foley, a Detroit police officer in Los Angeles on a case, is a rare example of a black detective who has two white sidekicks, in the roles of detective Billy Rosewood (Judge Reinhold) and John Taggart (John Ashton). Significantly, Rosewood and Taggart are not there to assist Foley but, rather, to keep an eye on him due to his unorthodox techniques. In most films, the black police detective's sidekick is often a white woman—as in *The Pelican Brief* (Alan J. Pakula, 1993), *Kiss the Girls* (Gary Fleder, 1997), *Murder at 1600* (Dwight H. Little, 1997), and *The Bone Collector* (Phillip Noyce, 1999). On the basis of the impression created by these films, as well as others, the black detective must be "negotiated" by either a white woman or a chaperone—as if not to alienate potential white audiences by making him appear too threatening or accomplished. This dynamic is quite different from the countless examples in which the white lead detective has a black sidekick to assist in case solving, where the sidekick is anything but a chaperone. One memorable example is the character of Sergeant Al Powell (Reginald VelJohnson), who can barely perform as a cop but somehow rediscovers his masculinity as a result of assisting the white and invincible John McClane (Bruce Willis) in *Die Hard* (John McTiernan, 1988).

While the tendency of casting the racial/ethnic/sexual other as villain or sidekick does not allow for many African American detectives and even fewer African American private eyes, it also enhances the private eye's status as an outsider the few times it does occur. Even more of an outsider than the typical white private eye, the African American private eye needs to negotiate a world that is already prejudiced against him for the color of his skin. Just as outsider status benefits the white private eye, providing a perspective unfettered by loyalties, the black detective can have greater perspective thanks to his status as even more of an outsider.

Several interesting racial dynamics play out over the seven seasons of *The Shield* that reinforce a similar sort of treatment. While Mackey and the members of his team are all white, it is detective Claudette Wyms (C. C. H. Pounder), an African American woman, who represents the voice of integrity and moral authority on the show. Isolated twice over (as a racial minority and a gendered minority), Wyms is conspicuously different on the show with regard not only to appearance but also to attitude. She repeatedly puts her career on the line, refusing to compromise her own moral code. Throughout much of the show's run, she is either an active antagonist or a passive antagonist to the misadventures of Mackey and his crew. She eventually forfeits an opportunity to be the new captain because she refuses to ignore the possible impact of a public defender's drug use on countless cases. While there is another African American on the department's force, Julien Lowe (Michael Jace), his role is smaller and more preoccupied with personal internal battles. At the same time, it is also clear that he too does not fit in with the mostly white police force.

It is not just that the hard-boiled private eye is often white but that his entire world is (for the most part) equally white. Roger A. Berger observes that "blacks have virtually no presence in Chandler's L.A. novels," despite the fact that "the presence of African-Americans was dramatically increasing in 1940s' and eventually 1950s' LA" (284). For the most part, private-detective films and literature barely acknowledge a black presence in Los Angeles, and if they do, as in *L.A. Confidential*, it is as victims to be investigated or framed by white police.

This is especially ironic because the inspiration for Sam Spade and Philip Marlowe was supposedly the real-life black private detective Samuel Marlowe. Referred to as the first black private detective west of the Mississippi in his obituary, Marlowe is said to have corresponded for years with both Raymond Chandler and Dashiell Hammett, neither of them realizing that he was black until they finally met in person (Ransil). Daniel Miller, in an article for the *Los Angeles Times*, describes "Nightshade," a four-page story that is Hammett's only work to feature a black protagonist. Marlowe's cache of letters from Hammett included a copy of "Nightshade" with a personal note from Hammett suggesting that Marlowe had inspired the story. Marlowe also did some detective work for Chandler and acted as a guide during "research expeditions" to the "tough parts of town" (D. Miller). In November 2016, the CW network announced that it was developing a period crime drama inspired by Samuel Marlowe, but that project never got off the ground.

The difficulty in getting Samuel Marlowe—or any other black private eye—on television should come as no surprise. In November 2017, *Variety* published the results of a study examining race in television writing rooms. The study found that only 35 percent of writers rooms for the

2016–2017 season had a black writer on staff, and within that 35 percent, fewer than 5 percent were black. Across the eighteen networks examined, the study found that 91 percent of showrunners were white, and 80 percent were men. In 17 percent of the writers rooms that did employ a single black writer, "that writer is often excluded from influencing the creative process and passed over for advancement," with AMC, CBS, and the CW labeled as the worst on "overall inclusion" when considering both race and gender (Turchiano). According to an analysis conducted by *Variety* of the new broadcast television shows for the 2017–2018 season, nothing changed. Specifically, Daniel Holloway outlines that of the lead actors, "only 20% were Hispanic or non-white, and only 35% were female," while of the showrunners, "10% were non-white or Hispanic and 29% were female."

EASY RAWLINS

In a sea of white private eyes (if not a sea of white leading men), Easy Rawlins stands out. He is the black protagonist in a series of novels and short stories set in Los Angeles during the 1940s through the 1960s, by the author Walter Mosley. Rawlins is very much an atypical L.A. private eye and not only because of his skin tone. A World War II veteran living in the South L.A. neighborhood of

Watts, Rawlins, for most of the novels, is an unlicensed and untrained private detective. Unlike his jaded and world-weary counterparts, Rawlins can be a bit naïve and inexperienced, and he does not own a gun. And, unlike many of his peers, Rawlins owns his house.

Walter Mosley's first published book, *Devil in a Blue Dress*, was also the first novel in his Easy Rawlins series. The film adaptation, starring Denzel Washington as Easy and directed by Carl Franklin, was released in 1995, five years after the book's release. It was a box-office disappointment, despite the success of the original book, critical praise, and the star power of Washington. Ed Guerrero suggests that the film's failure had to do with its release shortly after the O. J. Simpson trial and the heightened racial tensions that resulted from it (qtd. in Gates 213). However, Leon Lewis suggests that another reason for the film's lack of commercial success could be the absence of a white sidekick (qtd. in Gates 213).

Mosley frequently comments on the racism and injustice experienced by many African Americans, an issue rarely raised in other hard-boiled detective narratives. The film critic James Berardinelli writes about *Devil in a Blue Dress*, "As the film progresses, it becomes evident that skin color is more than a background issue—it's the first thing anyone notices, and can break careers, shatter marriages, and end lives." Both the book and film versions of *Devil in a Blue Dress*, as well as Mosley's work as a whole, demonstrate how the genre of the private detective can provide an opportunity for exploring evolutions of racial prejudice throughout the United States' twentieth century.

Devil in a Blue Dress is set in a postwar Los Angeles uncertain about the influx of African Americans who had moved westward searching for work in war-related industries. As Rawlins himself explains in the film, "Black people from the south moved to California to get the good jobs in the shipyards and the aircraft companies." It was from one of these jobs that Rawlins is fired for insubordination. Even though he has no training or experience as a detective, Rawlins—desperate for any kind of work—accepts a job searching for Daphne Monet (Jennifer Beals), a white woman known to frequent the black jazz clubs of South Central Los Angeles. However, much like in other hard-boiled narratives, this case is not as simple as it seems. The plot thickens as Rawlins discovers layers of corruption and intrigue and even gets implicated in two murders, while searching for—and eventually finding—Monet, who turns out to be Ruby, an African American woman passing as white. By the end of the movie, Rawlins, perhaps emboldened by his success, decides to open his own private investigation business.

Unlike traditional hard-boiled novels, in which social divides tend to be demarcated by wealth (or lack thereof), Mosley sets up social divides based on race. Much as Philip Marlowe is noteworthy for his ability to traverse class lines in Los Angeles, Rawlins is noteworthy for his ability to traverse lines of race despite his blackness, rendering him well suited for the task of tracking down Monet. For instance, when Monet calls Rawlins, inviting him to her hotel, she tells him that he must slip into the white section of the hotel in order to find her, which he is able to do but not without reservation. Later that night, when Rawlins drives Monet home, they pass a police car. Monet asks Rawlins if he is nervous. In voice-over, Rawlins tells us, "Nervous? Here I was in the middle of the night in a white neighborhood with a white woman in my car. Naw, I wasn't nervous. I was stupid." Stupid he may be, but he still manages to avoid attention.

The racial divide does not merely keep the blacks separate from the whites; it also keeps the whites separate from the blacks. As Rawlins explains, via voice-over, "Even though we had fought a war to keep the world free, the color line in America worked both ways, and even a rich white man like Todd Carter was afraid to cross it." Monet, who naively believes that Carter (Terry Kinney) can marry her now that he is certain to become mayor—thanks to the revelation that his opponent is a pedophile—Carter refuses to do so. Despite his love for Monet and his privileged status, he cannot marry someone who is partially black.

In the book *Little Scarlet* (2004), set in Los Angeles in the wake of the 1965 Watts riots, Rawlins has an office, which is where he is approached by the LAPD, which wants his assistance on a case. Aware of the hatred and distrust felt by the residents, white police officers do not want to wander through a smoldering Watts, and so police detective Melvin Suggs reaches out to Rawlins, asking him to find some answers. It is the specific connection that Rawlins has to his racially defined community that sets him apart from other (white) detectives.

There are many other nods to race in Mosley's work. For instance, in the novel *Black Betty*, published in 1994 and set in Los Angeles during the early 1960s, Rawlins is hired to find a missing black housekeeper, nicknamed Black Betty. When Rawlins visits a farm belonging to Albert Cain, Betty's employer, he observes that it reminds him of a slave plantation: "It's like I drove out of California, back through the south, and all the way into hell" (118). A few decades later, this is how Rawlins describes the racial divide of late-1960s Los Angeles in *Charcoal Joe* (2016):

> It's a long way from West L.A. to Watts. It's the same city but a darkness descends as you progress eastward. You pass

from white dreams into black and brown realities. There were many miles to cover but distance was the least of it. It was another world, where I was going. In West Los Angeles, when people looked at their TVs they saw themselves and what they wanted to be: James Arness and Lorne Green, Mary Tyler Moore and Lucille Ball. . . . People in Watts saw the same shows but not their faces, their dreams, the hard facts of their lives. In Watts, people spoke the same language in different dialects and at separate schools. For darker-skinned citizens *employment* was synonymous with *toil*. The police were often the enemy. (39)

In *Devil in a Blue Dress*, it is clear that the police are the enemy. Not only do they beat up Rawlins, for no reason at all, but they threaten to frame him. One of the cops tells Rawlins that they will send a team over to look through his house and that they will definitely find something to implicate Rawlins in the murder of Richard McGee (Scott Lincoln), not to mention the murder of Coretta James (Lisa Nicole Carson). As the second cop says to Rawlins in true Vic Mackey style, "Evidence has a funny way of showing up, you know?"

Because the police are often seen as the enemy, Rawlins spends a lot of time helping people who turn to him rather than the police. Berardinelli observes that the most interesting element of the film is not the "whodunit" but the "whydunit": the search for the guilty parties is less interesting than "learning their motivation, which is buried in society's perception of racial interaction." Seeing the world through Rawlins's eyes, through his perspective as a black detective, reminds us of these perceptions. Rawlins sees a world that few others can see, much less understand.

Another difference between Rawlins and the hard-boiled detective is the amount of sexual activity depicted in the film. Unlike the more isolated private eye, who either avoids sexual activity outright or limits it to rare occasions, Rawlins is far more sexually prolific. Mosley can be quite graphic about these exploits, not only emphasizing the stereotype of the overly sexualized black male but even being critical of it. While gathering information on Daphne, Easy meets up with her friend Coretta. Philippa Gates points out that "Easy thinks that by having sex with Coretta he will discover the information he wants regarding Daphne. But as the sexual act occurs we see that Easy is desperate for sex and at Coretta's mercy, quite literally, giving her information in return for sexual gratification. His sexuality then becomes a weakness rather than a strength, and he admits as much in his voice-over" (211).

In contrast, Philip Marlowe finds it all too simple to reject a woman's advances. In *The Big Sleep*, when Vivian invites him to come home with her following a kiss in his car, he tells her, "Kissing is nice, but your father didn't hire me to sleep with you" (130). He drops a sulking Vivian off at her house before heading home to discover a naked Carmen in his bed. "That's nice," he tells her, "but I've already seen it all" (133). When she refuses to get dressed, he thinks to himself, "It's so hard for women—even nice women—to realize that their bodies are not irresistible" (134). It might be hard for an average man to resist either of the two women, but for Marlowe, it is just another day's work.

Despite Rawlins's sexual aggressions, he is remarkably nonviolent. In *Devil in a Blue Dress*, the violence is delegated to his friend Mouse Alexander (Don Cheadle) to perform. It is as though the notion of an "angry black man" is too intense for the film's protagonist. So Rawlins maintains his thoughtfulness, patience, and physical restraint, leaving it to Mouse to do the shooting and punching. When Mouse kills Joppy (Mel Winkler), the only explanation is that Mouse did not have time to tie Joppy up. "If you didn't want him killed, why did you leave him with me?" he asks Rawlins without any hint of apology. Despite the fact that the hard-boiled detective usually has to resort to the occasional violence as an occupational hazard, Rawlins generally avoids it. For instance, when DeWitt Albright (Tom Sizemore) and his crew break into Rawlins's home and threaten him, it is Mouse who defends Rawlins before more damage can be done.

Another crucial aspect of Rawlins's character is his home ownership. Not only does it set him apart from others in his neighborhood, indicating an aspersion to conventional middle-class values, but it makes him a tangible part of his community, very different from the stereotypical hard-boiled detective who belongs nowhere. When Rawlins's home first appears in the *Devil in a Blue Dress* movie, he says, via voice-over, "I loved coming home to my house. . . . I guess maybe I just loved owning something." Whatever troubles have plagued him along the way, the very end of the film shows Rawlins to be at peace. "I sat with my friend on my porch at my house, and we laughed a long time," he says, via voice-over. The emphasis is on the possession: *my* friend, *my* porch, *my* house. This possession anchors Rawlins in a way not commonly seen by a private eye. His house represents his roots not only in California but in his neighborhood, among his community, a community that he will continue to assist with his new detective agency.

Rawlins's home is doubly significant because he does not have an office. Unlike most private eyes, who are rarely at home, he uses his home as his base, indicating just how unable he is to extricate himself from a case once he accepts it. However, in spite of the fact that he owns his house—a rare feat for a black man of that time period—Rawlins still maintains a degree of isolation from the community around him, an isolation further compounded when he leaves his black neighborhood to venture into white territory.

The African American detective became a more popular figure in contemporary film, especially in the 1990s—although he almost always was a police detective, as in Eddie Murphy's portrayal of the renegade police detective Axel Foley in the hugely successful *Beverly Hills Cop* (Martin Brest, 1984). There were three sequels, one in 1987 (directed by Tony Scott), another in 1994 (directed by John Landis), and a third currently in development. Morgan Freeman played the soon-to-be-retiring police detective William Somerset in *Seven* (David Fincher, 1995), as well as the detective and forensic psychologist Alex Cross in *Kiss the Girls* (1997) and its sequel, *Along Came a Spider* (Lee Tamahori, 2001). In 1993, two years before *Devil in a Blue Dress* was released, Denzel Washington played the investigative reporter Gray Grantham in *The Pelican Brief,* while in 1999, he played the forensics expert Lincoln Rhyme in *The Bone Collector,* as well as the corrupt narcotics officer Alonzo Harris in *Training Day* (Fuqua, 2001). Wesley Snipes was the retired U.S. Secret Service agent John Cutter in *Passenger 57* (Kevin Hooks, 1992) and the Metropolitan Police homicide detective

Harlan Regis in *Murder at 1600* (Dwight H. Little, 1997). Sidney Poitier was FBI Deputy Director Carter Preston in *The Jackal* (Caton-Jones, 1997), and Samuel L. Jackson played Zeus Carver, the reluctant partner of John McClane (Bruce Willis) in *Die Hard with a Vengeance* (John McTiernan, 1993), as well as a hostage lieutenant in *The Negotiator* (F. Gary Gray, 1998) and NYPD Detective John Shaft II in *Shaft* (John Singleton, 2000), a sequel to the 1971 film of the same name (Gates 192–193). Black police detectives were also featured in television shows such as *Homicide: Life on the Street* (NBC, 1993–1999), *Law & Order: Special Victims Unit* (NBC, 1999–present), *The Shield* (FX, 2002–2008), *The Wire* (HBO, 2002–2008), and *Detroit 1-8-7* (ABC, 2010–2011).

While there are many examples, on both the large and small screens, of black police detectives, black private eyes still remain few and far between. One rare example that provides an interesting contrast to *Devil in a Blue Dress* is the film *Shaft* (Gordon Parks, 1971), about John Shaft (Richard Roundtree), a black private detective in New York City. Much like Marlowe in Los Angeles, Shaft traverses the island of Manhattan, from his home in Greenwich Village to his office in midtown and in and around Harlem. Unlike Rawlins, however, Shaft is a licensed private investigator. Because of Rawlins's lack of credibility—he has no license, for starters—he must rely on the support of Todd Carter (Terry Kinney), a white civic leader who will most likely be the next mayor of Los Angeles. Shaft has no such allegiances.

Regardless of the differences, there is a key similarity between Mosley's narratives and others in the detective genre until the advent of neo-noir. They are fundamentally reassuring, in spite of the corruption and crime that happen along the way. Mosley, like Chandler before him, emphasizes the existence of an unwavering moral code that proves resilient against those who abuse or ignore it. The world may still be flawed, but for a moment, we are reminded that there are good people who do good things, even if we find them in unexpected places or in unexpected people.

5

THE LADY DICK

I don't know anything about women.
— Sam Spade, in *The Maltese Falcon*

One or two authors have experimented with the woman
detective, but for the most part with little success.
— Marjorie Hope Nicolson,
"The Professor and the Detective"

THE FEMALE PROBLEM

With men leaving to fight in Europe during World War II,
American women entered the workplace in record numbers. However, once the men returned home, the inte-
gration of women in the workplace—and in jobs that
had previously been reserved for these men—became
an issue. The ensuing anxieties about the dangers of
overly independent and assertive women—and their
corresponding threats to masculinity—had impact both
on and offscreen. It was no coincidence that the femme

fatale, Hollywood's lethal siren, emerged in sync with this postwar readjustment and that the hard-boiled private eye's success would routinely come as a direct result of just how well he kept her at bay.

Women in detective narratives traditionally serve two purposes: either to complicate the detective's mission (as an object of sexual desire and/or as a participant in the corrupt or criminal enterprise) or to help in the afore-mentioned mission, as a resource or as an assistant. Occa-sionally, they serve a third purpose: the villain. Therefore, it is paramount for the detective to keep the woman at arm's length—regardless of which role she plays—in order to demonstrate his own self-control, integrity, and independence. She can be a criminal, she can be a victim, but she will always have the potential to be a dangerous distraction.

In contrast to traditional detectives, such as Hercule Poirot or Sherlock Holmes, who are often seen as being less masculine because of their embrace of certain effem-inate cultural and intellectual pursuits, the hard-boiled detective is seen as thoroughly tough and masculine. This is why having a female equivalent is out of the ques-tion or, at the very least, problematic. In fact, when our hard-boiled private eye first emerged, there was literally no precedent "for a tough-talking, worldly-wise woman, capable of defending herself in the roughest company, who also possessed the indispensable heroic qualities of physical attractiveness and virtue" (Porter, *Pursuit* 183). As a result of the required characteristics, the hard-boiled detective simply *had* to be a man. David Glover even argues that the hard-boiled tradition can be viewed "as a masculine reclaiming of the detective novel, which was seen as overly feminized, dominated by detectives who were female (Miss Marple, Harriet Vane) or insufficiently masculine (Hercule Poirot, Peter Wimsey)" (Shuker-Haines and Umphrey 71).

This type of gender preference is not limited to detective novels, of course. American movies, television shows, and popular fiction often feel aggressively male. Qualities such as "bad grammar, slang, . . . cussing, blaspheming, hard drinking," have long been seen not only as the prerogatives of men and boys but also as "defensive reactions against the encroachments of civilizing womankind and the tyranny of hearth and home" (Porter, *Pursuit* 184). This kind of language and behavior is a resilient celebration of masculinity, the verbal equivalent of beating a drum in the forest, a retaliation against all cultural and intellectual pursuits coded feminine. In contrast, if a woman is associated with any such thing, it can make her seem crude, vulgar, or cheap.

The masculinity of detective heroes, in particular, was reinforced in the 1920s and 1930s on the pages of

Black Mask, where the stories were known to be violent and dark. The editor Joseph T. Shaw, in an attempt to attract female readers, proposed to the writer Erle Stanley Gardner—who went on to create the lucrative Perry Mason franchise—that the magazine add "a touch of feminine interest that would not let down . . . he-man readers and would at the same time bring in a swarm of new ones of both genders." However, when Gardner responded by suggesting the writer Nell Martin—"That girl can create a female detective that'll hit dead center with *Black Mask* readers"—Shaw clarified that he had been misunderstood. He was only suggesting that Gardner add female *characters* to his stories, he said. *Black Mask* "is by no manner going to be feminine" (qtd. in Walton 175).

Therefore, it should come as little surprise that the identity of the hard-boiled detective has masculinity as a prerequisite. And during those rare moments when a bold writer or director attempts to reconfigure expectations by putting a female where a male would otherwise be? More often than not, this noble attempt fails outright—with either critical or commercial failure or both. At the very least, the persona of the private detective has to be significantly reinvented to accommodate the extra estrogen.

Due to women's alleged proficiency for gossip and intuition, they can be good amateur detectives—such as J. B. Fletcher (Angela Lansbury) from the long-running television crime drama *Murder, She Wrote* (CBS, 1984–1996) or Agatha Christie's Miss Marple—but not professional private eyes. The amateur is given more room for error, and luck is given more credit than actual skill. Mistakes are more easily forgiven—if not expected—and successes are more easily dismissed. The amateur, innately comfortable in the domestic sphere, is also naturally suited for "cleaning up" crimes that have disturbed the peaceful home.

In contrast, the job of the professional detective requires attributes traditionally seen as masculine, such as courage, independence, strength, and experience. With these abilities, the professional detective can boldly leave the domestic sphere, traversing the urban expanse in pursuit of clues and criminals. This would be, to quote the title of the 1972 detective novel by the author P. D. James, an unsuitable job for a woman. After all, while an amateur detective can contend with a peaceful home that is temporarily destabilized by the actions of a particular troublemaker, an urban expanse that is riddled with crime, corruption, and transgressive behavior is no match for her.

It is not merely that the demands of the job require characteristics that are commonly deemed masculine but that female qualities themselves are contradictory to the necessary elements of the detective formula, argues

Kathleen Gregory Klein in her book *The Woman Detective: Gender and Genre*. Klein writes that while success feels natural "when the detective is professional and paid for his work," this only works when the detective is a man. If the paid detective is a woman, "this anticipated pattern of successful crime solving suddenly collapses" (1). The issue, as Klein explains it, is that the detective narrative creates fear and tension, both of which are assuaged as a result of the detective's success at solving the mystery, identifying and capturing the criminal, and restoring order (4). The type of character who does these things— who solves problems and restores order—is traditionally masculine, as based on Joseph Campbell's hero cycle. A classic example is the character of Luke Skywalker (Mark Hamill) in *Star Wars* (George Lucas, 1977). The strong man, called to adventure, faces whatever trials or ordeals necessary in order to save the weak woman and/or the weak people before returning victorious. This is the basis for almost every Hollywood action narrative.

Therefore, when the detective is a woman, it destabilizes the traditional narrative structure, and it does so in ways that are inherently problematic. The detective must be strong (to rescue victims), intelligent (to solve the mystery), and able to traverse the geography of Los Angeles, both the homes of the rich and the gang-infested streets, unlike the woman who is most at home (literally and metaphorically) in the domestic arena. Having the hero be a woman pushes off center the "male/female, public/private, intellect/emotion, physical strength/ weakness dichotomy" that is at the heart of the detective narrative; the only way to restore order is by demonstrating that she is either "an incompetent detective" or "an inadequate woman" (K. Klein 4, 5). To be an adequate woman, of course, means to be happily married, to have children, *and* to have a tidy house—three qualities that seem impossible to achieve by any private detective. A man's masculinity, by contrast, is not invalidated by the mess of his apartment or by his lack of a spouse or children.

V. I. WARSHAWSKI

If a woman is a successful private eye, like the character of *V. I. Warshawski* in the movie of the same name, directed by Jeff Kanew and released in 1991, countless jokes are made at her expense about how ludicrous her career choice is, with such questions as, "You're a female dick, right?" or judgments such as, "You don't look much like a private detective to me." There are also cheap sexual jokes such as, "He hired me to look after his sausage," delivered by Warshawski (Kathleen Turner) herself, or "you're a lady dick," delivered to her.

In the movie, as well as in the books by Sue Paretzky on which the film is based, Warshawski refers to herself as "V. I." or "Vic," rather than her full name, Victoria Iphigenia. Those who are oblivious (or explicitly hostile) to her gender neutrality call her "Vicki" (Shuker-Haines and Umphrey 72). She is also told repeatedly what a poor excuse for a woman she is, and the movie makes this visually clear. Her apartment is filthy, the refrigerator is full of moldy food, there are no clean dishes, and there is nowhere to sit. When one of her visitors looks in the fridge, she exclaims, "Eww! Jesus! This is disgusting." Warshawski's superior, Detective Lieutenant Bobby Mallory (Charles Durning), tells her, point black, "being a detective is no job for a girl like you," and he suggests that if her father had been more of a disciplinarian, she would have become a happy housewife.

Even Warshawski's potential maternal qualities are called into question. When Mallory hears that she is looking for a little girl, his reply is, "Since when do you care about kids?" Warshawski herself worries about her lack of maternal qualities, asking—in all seriousness and from the depths of self-doubt—"Do you think I'd be a good mother?" It is as if to be truly successful, she must also be a good mother. No other type of success is equivalent.

In the books, in contrast, Warshawski, the daughter of a cop, is seen as "a no-nonsense, fairly noncerebral, baseball-loving woman in her mid-thirties, ... solid, down to earth, almost blue-collar although she specializes in white-collar cases" (Baker and Nietzel 322). She becomes a detective almost by chance, resigning her position as a public defender in Chicago to investigate a robbery charge against a friend's brother. The choice to be an investigator is a calling that comes out of responsibility. Not only is the book version of Warshawski not losing sleep wondering if she would be a good mother, but Warshawski describes herself as "a lousy housewife," a label with which she is comfortable. Divorced after a fourteen-month marriage, she explains that her foray into marriage was brief due to the fact that "some men can only admire independent women at a distance" (Paretsky 37). This does not seem to bother her.

However, the film *V. I. Warshawski*, loosely based on the Sue Paretsky novel *Deadlock*, turns this toughness into a joke—the alternate title for the film, used for some of the international releases, is *V. I. Warshawski: Detective in High Heels*. The film also questions Warshawski's lack of maternal proclivities, emphasizing the ideal of the nuclear family in a way entirely lacking in the original book. In the film, Warshawski (Kathleen Turner) meets the former hockey star Boom-Boom Grafalk (Stephen Meadows) at her local bar, and they go home together. When Grafalk is murdered shortly thereafter, Warshawski agrees to watch his daughter, Kat (Angela Goethals), while tracking down the killer. The character of the child does not even exist in the book. Throughout the movie, as Warshawski both babysits and investigates the murder, a child is her sidekick. Not only does the film imply that Warshawski needs Kat's help to obtain necessary information, but it demeans Warshawski by implying that this is the sidekick she deserves. By the end of the film, Warshawski and her friend Murray (Jay O. Sanders) become surrogate parents for Kat, as if acknowledging that only now Warshawski can be complete.

Despite the fact that Warshawski (the detective) is successful, in that she solves the case and rescues the girl, *V. I. Warshawski* (the movie) was not. Originally intended to be part of a franchise that capitalized on the success of the book series, the film's critical and commercial failure guaranteed that no others were made. In contrast to the empowered feminist created by Paretsky, the film version is a caricature who complains about her weight, going jogging after a disappointing readout on her scale, for instance. In contrast, the book version of Paretsky is more concerned with trying to bulk up. By adding the character of Kat Grafalk, the film also forces Warshawski to display a maternal side completely at odds with her literary counterpart. The celluloid Warshawski destabilizes the binary by trying to play both sides. She is strong but also wants to lose weight, she is tough but also maternal, she is smart but also emotional, she pursues bad guys but also wants to have a kid, she is capable but needs assistance. While a real-life person could balance all these characteristics, the broad strokes of Hollywood cliché leave us with a confusing and contradictory caricature. And a sequel would have been even worse. The second film intended to depict Warshawski in the throes of a midlife crisis, "deciding to settle down and have a child of her own" (Mizejewski 140).

While *V. I. Warshawski* is set in Chicago, rather than Los Angeles, the reason for its inclusion here is both simple and sad. There are very few female private eyes, and out of the ones that exist, even fewer actually solve cases on their own. Warshawski is such an exception that it is worth mentioning her, even if—or perhaps *because*—the film was such a failure. Not only is the typical loner private investigator such an anomaly that a female version is difficult to find, but when one does find her, she is not even in the right city.

While it may not subvert the detective genre entirely to make the detective female, it does provide various complications that call into question much about contemporary America's gender roles and stereotypes. As Kathleen Gregory Klein describes, the detective narrative is built on binaries: good versus evil, victim versus criminal, detective versus criminal. While a certain amount of blur-ring is permitted (the detective can do bad things pro-vided he has good intentions, much as the criminal can do good things but with bad intentions), if the binary is pushed too far, it will break. Therefore, the detective can have some feminine qualities—he can have empathy, for example—but he must be inherently masculine. He must be more masculine than empathetic. This masculinity becomes a nonnegotiable part of the detective's persona and allows him to assert his dominance over the narra-tive, over the criminal(s), and over his female colleagues, regardless of whether they are subservient or threatening. Dominance, after all, reads as a masculine quality. There-fore, the hero, by the end of the narrative, is deemed suc-cessful as a direct result of his dominance. This is why Jake Gittes is so emasculated by the end of *Chinatown* (Roman Polanski, 1974). His failure is demonstrated by the fact that he is not dominant over anyone and, in fact, is dominated by Noah Cross. Submission reads as a feminine quality, and so only criminals and women (and failed detectives) return to their "proper, secondary places" (K. Klein xi).

The dangerous woman, who knows too much and deceives too often, must be defeated by our detective, or at least domesticated, by the end of the narrative. Evelyn Mulwray may have had power and agency through part of *Chinatown*, but by the end, she has been so thoroughly dominated that she is dead. Noah Cross has dominated her. In *L.A. Confidential* (James Ellroy, 1997), Officer Wendell "Bud" White (Russell Crowe) domesticates the formerly sexy prostitute Lynn Bracken (Kim Basinger), riding off into the sunset with her, most likely toward a future of children and a house in the suburbs.

BIMBOS, BABES, AND PRIVATE EYES

I do not mean to imply that the detective is never a female or that if she is, it is always as problematic as *V. I. Warshawski*. However, if the detective *is* a female, her femininity is either minimized (in favor of her masculine characteristics), as in *V. I. Warshawski*, or amplified (making her into a camp-like figure, with high heels and exaggerated eyelashes). For instance, the blond and blue-eyed character of Honey West, created for a series of books by G. G. Fickling (an intentionally gender-ambiguous pseudonym referring to Forrest E. "Skip" Fickling) is described as "delicious," "luscious," and "voluptuous," and her "38-22-36 body is always being liberated from the swimming suits, negligee, and miniskirts she wears" (Baker and Nietzel 308). Readers are frequently reminded of her exact measurements. Book titles for the Honey West series include such salacious titles as *Girl on the Loose* (1958), *Honey in the Flesh* (1959), *Kiss for a Killer*

(1960), and *Bombshell* (1964). The cover of *This Girl for Hire* (1956) even declares, "The Return of the Nerviest, Curviest P.I. in Los Angeles!" The television series based on the book—starring Anne Francis as Honey West— aired on ABC from 1965 to 1966, and it was the first regular series with a female detective. Or, as the website *Thrilling Detective* declares, "The first really successful female private eye in a series was a bimbo!" (Smith).

Forrest told the *Los Angeles Times* in 1986 that the inspiration for the character Honey West came from actress Marilyn Monroe and the character Mike Hammer, a hardboiled detective created by the author Mickey Spillane: "I decided to put the two together.... We thought the most used name for someone you really like is Honey. And she lives in the West, so there was her name" (qtd. in McLellan). Her personality is similarly simplistic. West inherits a Los Angeles detective agency from her late father and stumbles into a career of detection as a way of finding his killer, much as Warshawski does.

Lest one think West is too independent, her partner, Johnny—renamed Sam Bolt (John Ericson) for the TV series—frequently swoops to her rescue. Bolt routinely rescues West when her various antics leave her beaten up in an alley, knocked out with a tranquilizer gun, or kidnapped by international art thieves. He does more than rescue her, however. He also chastises her when he thinks her behavior is out of line. For example, in the opening minutes of "Live a Little, Kill a Little," he shouts at her for having accepted a case without consulting him. While West does, occasionally, hold her own, at the very end of the pilot episode—"The Swingin' Mrs. Jones" (ABC, September 17, 1965)—Aunt Meg (Irene Hervey) cautions West, "You know, there's one thing you must understand, Honey. You have to let the man win once in a while." West's reply? "Believe me, Aunt Meg, you're looking at a sore loser."

The character of Honey West was introduced to television audiences in an episode of *Burke's Law* (ABC, 1963–1966), a detective series featuring Gene Barry as Police Captain Amos Burke, the millionaire captain of the LAPD's homicide division. In that episode, "Who Killed the Jackpot?" (April 21, 1965), West is described as the "private eyeful." As she gets into Burke's chauffeur-driven Rolls Royce, she asks, "Do they make these in pink for lady detectives?" It is not clear if she is joking. In the same episode, Sam Bolt is presented as West's watchdog "with no leash." Even though Francis won a Golden Globe and was nominated for an Emmy for her role as Honey West, the show was canceled after one year. Despite Reese Witherspoon's interest in bringing West to the big screen more recently, the project never moved forward.

Another example of an overly feminized female detective is Alison B. Gordon, created by the writer Walter Wager for a trio of books published between 1979 and 1981 (*Blue Leader*, *Blue Moon*, and *Blue Murder*). Rather than transitioning from a career as a private detective to being an agent with the CIA, as Honey West eventually does, Gordon is a former CIA agent who becomes a private investigator based in Los Angeles. In *Private Eyes: One Hundred and One Knights*, Robert A. Baker and Michael T. Nietzel describe Gordon as a "very beautiful, $400-a-day, Beverly Hills private eye, a ritzy female combination of James Bond and Stanley Ellin's John Milano. . . . She is a widow in her thirties and when she meets a man she likes, she makes love to him several times a day" (325). That is not all she does to men, however. Both femme fatale *and* private eye, Gordon boasts, "I've used them, fooled them, exposed them, analyzed them, laid them, . . . and killed them" (qtd. in Baker and Nietzel 325).

Interestingly, Warshawski, West, and Gordon have no problem sleeping around, seemingly having sex more often than Philip Marlowe. Is this a way to make them appear more masculine? Or is it a way to make them appear more feminine? A study of sexual and violent content by gender in the 855 top-grossing U.S. films released from 1950 to 2006 found not only that were there two male characters for every female character but that female characters were twice as likely to have sex as male characters were (Bleakley, Jamieson, and Romer 73). Clearly, it is impossible to imagine a female detective who is not interested in sex. It is as if, by being willing to spread her legs, the female detective renders herself both physically and mentally available and therefore less threatening and more accessible. By wielding her sexuality without shame and sometimes even as a weapon—such as Brigid O'Shaughnessy (Mary Astor) in *The Maltese Falcon* (John Huston, 1941) or Phyllis Dietrichson (Barbara Stanwyck) in *Double Indemnity* (Billy Wilder, 1944)—she demonstrates that, whatever the superficial differences in power and responsibility between men and women, a woman is best suited to play the femme fatale.

Another way to emphasize the female detective's vulnerabilities is to make sure that she cannot succeed on her own. In Denise Hamilton's novel *The Last Embrace*, published in 2008 but set in 1949, the protagonist, Lily Kessler, is an American spy during World War II who comes to Los Angeles to find her late fiancé's sister, Kitty, an actress whose body is found below the Hollywood sign. In typical hard-boiled fashion, the police are useless, and Kessler must forge her own way through Hollywood actresses and gangsters in search of the truth. Unfortunately, despite her stellar qualifications, Kessler must rely on the assistance of a stubborn homicide detective not only to find the truth but to survive.

REMINGTON STEELE

A female private eye needing the assistance of a male to succeed is the underlying gimmick for the television show *Remington Steele* (NBC, 1982–1987). An ingenious commentary on American sexism and misogyny, the basic concept behind the show is that, quite literally, a female private eye cannot succeed without a man. Laura Holt, played by Stephanie Zimbalist, opens her own detective agency in Los Angeles; but no one shows up, and she is forced to close the office after a few months. As she explains in the show's opening credits, "I studied and apprenticed and put my name on an office, but absolutely nobody knocked down my door. A female private investigator seemed so . . . feminine." So what does she do? She invents a "decidedly masculine" superior—the fictional Remington Steele—and suddenly there are cases "around the block." Much to her surprise, however, an unnamed con man played by Pierce Brosnan turns up in the pilot episode, adopting the persona of Remington Steele as part of his strategy to steal some jewels that Holt is guarding. However, he flashes his baby blues and ends up joining the agency as the "actual" Remington Steele.

Holt and Steele establish a dynamic in which she does the work while he remains the public face of the company, since every successful detective agency needs a (white) man as its face.

Rather than ignoring the sexism at the show's core, *Remington Steele* makes frequent references to it. Even as it makes light of the repeated sexism that Holt faces, it still verbally addresses it, over and over. For example, Holt is frequently referred to as Steele's secretary, or even as the "second stringer" in the episode "Tempered Steele" (NBC, October 8, 1982), by those who do not know the true dynamic or refuse to believe it. Another device used in many episodes is for Steele to turn to Holt to ask how he solved the case, so that she can tell him how to explain "his" discovery publicly. The two of them are clearly aware each time of the question's ironic connotations.

In the show's pilot episode, "License to Steele" (NBC, October 1, 1982), Holt verbally acknowledges that, no matter how successful her efforts, the recognition is inevitably nil: "The lion's share of the credit always went to my male counterparts, regardless of their contribution." Pierce Brosnan, as the fake Steele, replies, "Tawdry thing, this male chauvinism." The topic of recognition is also addressed in the closing moments of "Tempered Steele," when Steele notices that Holt's name is not mentioned in any of the articles about their firm's latest success. Steele asks Holt if she noticed this, to which she replies, "One learns to live with it."

MOONLIGHTING

A version of the *Remington Steele* premise was used for the television show *Moonlighting* (ABC, 1985–1989), starring Bruce Willis as David Addison Jr. and Cybil Shepherd as Maddie Hayes. Unexpectedly bankrupt due to a faulty business manager, the former model Hayes joins one of her failing businesses that had been set up as a tax write-off, the Blue Moon Detective Agency. While every episode features a different case, the crux of the show was inevitably the dynamic between Addison and Hayes. Despite the fact that Hayes's character is consistently difficult, demanding, and tense, and despite the fact that she clearly owns the detective agency, there is no clear hierarchy between her and Addison. If anything, Addison is in charge, as evident in the show's second episode—"Gunfight at the So-So Corral" (March 5, 1985)—when he tells Hayes, "You are going to get such a licking when your father gets home," in response to her refusal to obey his orders. The fact that the show's creator, Glenn Gordon Caron, admits that the series had been inspired by a production of William Shakespeare's *The*

Taming of the Shrew (Caron) says all you need to know about the Hayes/Addison dynamic.

Whatever power Hayes may have as business owner is offset both by the way Addison treats her and by the persistent pastels she wears, preferably in satin. Hayes is often seen in shimmery pale pinks, pale blues, creams, and off-whites, all colors meant to soften and infantilize her, a condition exacerbated by her naiveté. In the episode "The Lady in the Iron Mask" (October 1, 1985), a downtrodden Hayes asks Addison why their work is not more fun, why solving their first legitimate case leaves her still feeling empty inside. A sardonic Addison replies that cashing the $5,000 paycheck will help fill her up. "That's what it's all about, isn't it?" Hayes asks, subdued. Addison, with just a touch of condescension, responds, "Welcome to the real world, Maddie Hayes." He also alludes to her naiveté in "The Dream Sequence Always Rings Twice" (October 15, 1985) after she complains that she does not like profiting from infidelity. "These kinds of cases are the backbone of the investigation business," Addison explains. "They are our bread and butter. . . . Infidelity is as American as apple pie. . . . Our business is built on a lack of trust." A few minutes later, Addison specifies why it is that Hayes has a hard time interpreting situations correctly: "You look at everything like a woman first and then a person second. . . . You don't look at a situation objectively. You don't look at a situation like an individual. You look at a situation like somebody appointed you guardian for your whole damn sex." Yet again, the message is how incompatible femininity is with detecting.

COPS AND AGENTS

Because of the difficulties in making a woman a private detective—since, heaven forbid, she might look at something from a female perspective—female detectives are often police officers or FBI agents, sometimes even lawyers or insurance investigators, buried in teams, networks, and bureaucracy. Anything but private eyes. For example, *Get Christie Love!* was both a made-for-television movie (ABC, January 22, 1974) and a short-lived television series (ABC, 1974–1975) featuring a black female police detective in New York City. As Christie, Teresa Graves was the first African American woman to star in an hour-long TV series. In 2017, ABC purchased *Get Christie Love*, a reboot of the original series, with Kylie Bunbury cast in the lead role, demonstrating the continued popularity of the trope, as well as the commercial viability of a black female police detective when compared to a black male private detective, such as Samuel Marlowe.

Other examples of female police detectives are Angie Dickinson's Pepper Anderson of *Police Woman* (NBC,

1975–1978), an undercover cop for the LAPD; *Cagney & Lacey* (CBS, 1982–1988), with Tyne Daly and Sharon Gless as two female police officers in New York City; and Lieutenant Olivia Benson (Mariska Hargitay) from the NYPD's Special Victims Unit on *Law & Order: SVU* (NBC, 1999–present), the longest-running prime-time drama currently on television. With regard to the female cop, there does not seem to be a huge difference between New York City and Los Angeles. Both are urban areas in which the cop struggles to maintain order more so than to unravel mysteries of any complexity.

Tellingly, films and shows with a female detective (either as part of a duo or as part of a police force) concern "themselves with examining the heroine's struggle as a woman in a man's world trying to balance a professional and personal life" (Gates 217–218). For instance, on *Law & Order: SVU*, Benson's career success is besieged with difficulties in her personal life, from her inability to sustain a relationship or have her own child (she adopts an orphaned baby she comes across during one her cases) to allegations of child abuse to a rocky relationship with that child's grandmother and then, in season 19, that same child's kidnapping.

On the big screen, mysteries have been solved by FBI agent in training Clarice Starling (Jodie Foster) in *The Silence of the Lambs* (Jonathan Demme, 1991), law student

Darby Shaw (Julia Roberts) in *The Pelican Brief* (Alan J. Pakula, 1993), lawyer Regina "Reggie" Love (Susan Sarandon) in *The Client* (Joel Schumacher, 1994), cop M. J. Monahan (Holly Hunter) in *Copycat* (Jon Amiel, 1995), police chief Marge Gunderson in *Fargo* (Joel and Ethan Coen, 1996), Secret Service agent Nina Chance (Diane Lane) in *Murder at 1600* (Dwight H. Little, 1997), police officer Amelia Donaghy (Angelina Jolie) in *The Bone Collector* (Phillip Noyce, 1999), insurance investigator Catherine Banning (Rene Russo) in *The Thomas Crown Affair* (John McTiernan, 1999), homicide detective Cassie Mayweather (Sandra Bullock) in *Murder by Numbers* (Barbet Schroeder, 2002), Interpol agent Alma Dray (Mélanie Laurent) in *Now You See Me* (Louis Leterrier, 2013), FBI Special Agent Sarah Ashburn (Sandra Bullock) and Boston police detective Shannon Mullins (Melissa McCarthy) in *The Heat* (Paul Feig, 2013), police detective Rhonda Boney (Kim Dickens) in *Gone Girl* (David Fincher, 2014), and police officer Rose Cooper (Reese Witherspoon) in *Hot Pursuit* (Anne Fletcher, 2015). This list may be long, but it is by no means inclusive. There are many more ladies in blue on both large and small screens, as well as female special agents, then there are female private eyes.

The list of female private detectives, in contrast, is remarkably short. And with few exceptions, the female private detective is usually paired with a man, as in *Remington Steele* or *Moonlighting* or *Honey West*. Why is this? Can the answer be as simple as that an independent woman, even in the twenty-first century, remains too threatening for Hollywood to imagine? Would audiences even watch if she were out there? Would *V. I. Warshawski* have been more of a success if she had not been turned into a joke? If she had not had to double as a babysitter? Women as part of a team—either in a partnership or on a police force—are less threatening.

CHARLIE'S ANGELS

For example, *Charlie's Angeles* (ABC, 1976–1981, as well as a few episodes in 2011, movies in 2000 and 2003, and a more recent reboot slated for a June 2019 release) is based on the premise that three women abandon careers in law enforcement when they find that all the opportunities available to them are severely limited by their gender. Instead, the three decide to pursue careers as private investigators for the Charles Townsend Agency. While "Charlie" (John Forsythe) exists—his voice frequently instructs Sabrina Duncan, Jill Munroe, and Kelly Garrett (originally played by Kate Jackson, Farrah Fawcett, Jaclyn Smith, respectively) on their cases—his face is never seen. His voice appears—via speakerphone—to give the women their assignments, and then they head off, usually undercover and unsupervised.

So while the agency is run by a male figurehead—who actually exists, unlike in *Remington Steele*—he is never seen and is completely hands-off once the ladies have their assignments. This device empowers the characters in a way that Holt in *Remington Steele* can never be empowered. However, at the same time, this empowerment is tempered by the title of the show—"Charlie's Angels" implies that the women are his property—the description of them as "little girls" in the opening credits, and the women's skimpy clothing; even Fawcett's explanation for the show's success is sobering: "When the show got to be Number Three, I figured it was our acting. When it got to be Number One, I decided it could only be because none of us wears a bra" (qtd. in Bennetts). Nonetheless, despite the scantily clad women, *Charlie's Angels* is a show about female camaraderie and teamwork. After all, women are supposed to work well with others. It is cowboys who ride off into the sunset alone.

CONVERTIBLES

Modern-day urban cowboys ride in big cars—Lincolns (*The Lincoln Lawyer*), Fords (*Chinatown*), Plymouths (*The Big Sleep*), Pontiacs (*Devil in a Blue Dress*), Chevrolets

(*L.A. Confidential*)—unless they are female. Or unless they are V. I. Warshawski, who drives a barely functional 1973 Plymouth Duster, an appropriately masculine car to convey how inadequately feminine she is. The first crop of televised male private eyes—Richard Diamond, Joe Mannix, and Matt Houston—also drove convertibles, fittingly, since the good looks and chiseled body were just as important as the ability to solve crimes (if not more so). What is the point in looking good if you cannot be looked *at*? These hunky private eyes had a lot in common with their female counterparts. The only male private eye in a convertible not exploiting his looks is *Chinatown*'s Jake Gittes, whose defeated and emasculated persona becomes increasingly clear as the film progresses. In his case, his car of choice sets him up for future vulnerabilities, both literal and metaphorical. It is more than likely that Evelyn Mulwray would not have been killed had she been driving a car with a proper roof. The car's open top leaves her exposed to the bullet.

Female private eyes not only drive smaller cars but are routinely behind the wheel of a convertible, exposed and on display, being looked at just as much as doing the looking (if not more so). For instance, Honey West drives a tiny, white two-seater convertible (a 1964 Shelby Cobra). Laura Holt drives a white VW Rabbit convertible as her personal car, unless she is with Remington, and then he drives—or they take the "company car" (a 1976 Cadillac Fleetwood), but Holt is never behind that wheel: Fred (Blake Clark), the company chauffeur, always drives. Veronica Mars, a female private eye in training from the television series *Veronica Mars* (UPN, 2004–2006; CW, 2007), drives a Chrysler Le Baron convertible. When Nancy Drew comes to Los Angeles in the 2007 movie directed by Andrew Fleming, her 1956 Nash Metropolitan convertible comes too. More recently, Alice Vaughan, in ABC's *The Catch* (2016) drives a sporty two-seater convertible (a 2015 Mercedes-Benz E 400).

THE CATCH

In March 2016, when ABC launched *The Catch*, starring Mireille Enos and produced by Shonda Rhimes, the powerhouse behind *Grey's Anatomy* (ABC, 2005–present) and *Scandal* (ABC, 2012–2018), all signs pointed to yet another success for Rhimes and ABC. The show was slickly produced and featured women at its core, both trademarks for Rhimes. Unfortunately, the show eked out only twenty episodes before being laid to rest by ABC.

The premise behind the show is *Remington Steele* with a twist. Mireille Enos plays Alice Vaughan, a tough, sexy, and *very* high-end (as evidenced by her incredible house, her expensive car, and the height of her stilettos) private investigator and a member of Vaughn and Associates. In the pilot episode, it is revealed that, despite the fact that Vaughan's job is to track down hackers, thieves, and con men, she has somehow remained oblivious to the fact that "Mr. X," a con man her agency has been struggling to identify, turns out to be the same man Vaughan is about to marry. Before she realizes this, he manages to steal $1.4 million from her, abandons her, and rips off another one of her clients. The fact that she is so betrayed seems barely a blip on the radar as Vaughan chases down her ex-fiancé, only to realize that she still loves him and he still loves her. Not only does she resume their relationship, but she begins involving him in her work.

A rare failure by Rhimes, *The Catch* will be remembered for two things: the inexplicable failure by a brilliant detective to realize that her fiancé is a con man (a metaphorical failure of vision) and her excessively heavy eyelashes (a literal obstruction of vision). *Vogue* described these eyelashes as "so outlandishly heavy that even Liza Minnelli might have balked" (Felsenthal). This description offers a deeper understanding of Alice Vaughan and how Shonda Rhimes and her team tried to make the female private eye work. With mile-high stilettos— hardly suited for the physical labor of investigation—and "outlandishly heavy" eyelashes, with sleek outfits and even sleeker car, Vaughan reads more as a femme fatale than a private eye. Significantly, she is not a bimbo, like Honey West, and she does not rely on a man to rescue her from repeated entanglements. She has no watchdog and, in fact, repeatedly defies her fiancé. She is not overly sexualized, like Alison B. Gordon. However, she is still very feminine, far more so than V. I. Warshawski (see the eyelashes, for example); but children are nowhere on the horizon, and even marriage seems like a miscalculation. Since a successful female private eye seems to remain as difficult to achieve as ever, Vaughan is a curious mix of femme fatale—although she does not get to use, fool, expose, or kill the man who stole everything from her— and leading lady. She is not a woman to be kept at bay. She may seem incapacitated by her heels and lashes, if not by her form-fitting attire, but at the same time, her agency has her name in the title, with no male figurehead, literal or symbolic.

Nonetheless, even when the private eye is black, as in the character of Easy Rawlins, he still seems to have more power than any female private eye discussed in this chapter—even if he has less commercial value in the eyes of television producers. Rawlins never needs rescuing, and he certainly is never shot with a tranquilizer gun. He does not entertain the notion of inventing a fake white man to be the figurehead for his new detective agency. He does not have $1.4 million stolen from him by a femme fatale with whom he later does business and continues a personal relationship. Enormous lashes or sky-high stilettos do not hobble him. He does not need children to help him gather information. Despite the fact that, in our perpetually racist society, a white woman may appear as higher on the racial hierarchy in certain circles, in the world of the L.A. private eye, she is an anomaly that must be tempered with good looks, high heels, and a team or a partner by her side.

6

THE GIRL SLEUTH

There is no clear sequence to the development of the girl detective heroine, but when Nancy Drew drove her blue roadster onto the scene in the early 1930s, the public was ready for her.

—Bobbie Ann Mason, *The Girl Sleuth: A Feminist Guide*

This girl, she's, uh, she's our age, and she's also a detective? Is she also a cartoon?

—Piz, in *Veronica Mars*

NANCY DREW

As inherently problematic as the female private eye can be, it is worth noting that there is one specific manifestation of the female private eye that is (marginally) less problematic: The girl sleuth. While the female private eye complicates and threatens the traditional hero/victim binary by adding feminine characteristics to the role of the hard-boiled private eye, the girl sleuth can add these same kinds of characteristics—empathy, sensitivity, femininity—while not posing a threat.

The girl sleuth rarely exists in Los Angeles or any big city, for that matter. She is more emblematic of the "cozy mysteries" common to the traditional detective narrative—in which a criminal anomaly upsets the tranquility of a small town—than of the urban corruption and pervasive criminality of the hard-boiled detective narrative. In this fashion, the iconic girl detective Nancy Drew solves mysteries as a hobby in her hometown of River Heights, a quaint fictional town somewhere in the U.S. Midwest. Nancy's assorted adventures—searching for missing family members or a lost inheritance, investigating a haunted house, tracking down a diary or precious jewel, looking into a case of mistaken identity—fill the pages of countless books, including those of the original *Nancy Drew Mystery Stories* series, launched in 1930, the *Nancy Drew Files*, launched in 1986, and the *Girl Detective* series, launched in 2004, plus five films, two television shows, numerous computer games, graphic novels, and even a podcast (*Unlocked! The Nancy Drew Podcast*).

Despite the fact that all the Nancy Drew books are written under the name "Carolyn Keene," there have been far too many for a single writer, no matter how driven. In fact, the Stratemeyer Syndicate, with Edward Stratemeyer at the helm, created the Nancy Drew machine. Edward

Stratemeyer would circulate outlines among his various staff writers, who would then fill in the details for a flat fee per book, with no royalties or other rights (Mason 7, 8). Inspired by the success of adult mysteries, the Stratemeyer Syndicate produced over a hundred different series, including the Bobbsey Twins, the Hardy Boys, Nancy Drew, and Tom Swift. Their mysteries were never about hard-hitting issues such as serial killers, corruption, or pedophilia. Rather, they were adventures to be enjoyed vicariously by children glued to the printed page, with titles such as *The Hidden Staircase* (1930), *The Clue in the Diary* (1932), and *The Secret of the Lost Lake* (1963).

The Stratemeyer Syndicate, under the pseudonym "Carolyn Keene," first published *The Secret of the Old Clock* in 1930, and sixteen-year-old Nancy was born. While the Hardy Boys may have been her masculine equivalent, there was no one else quite like Nancy. Before she emerged on the detective scene, girls solved mysteries in pairs or in groups. Sidekicks were viewed as essential, both for companionship and safety. While Nancy does have two friends (Bess Marvin and George Fayne) who often tag along, the mystery-solving domain is very much Nancy's alone. Ned Nickerson, her boyfriend, is superfluous at best. As the first independent girl sleuth, Nancy Drew and her blue sports car blazed a trail that others could only follow.

Bobbie Ann Mason, in her book *The Girl Sleuth: A Feminist Guide*, argues that "Nancy was popular precisely because of this blue car, which carried her into more dangerous situations than usually graced the pages of girls' books.... Readers have always been impressed with the way she backs her car 'skillfully' out of her driveway and 'maneuvers' into tight parking spaces" (16). The car—and Nancy's ability to drive it—became crucial to her initial mystique. At the time of Nancy's debut, owning a car was rare enough, much less driving one unchaperoned. Philippa Gates, in her book *Detecting Women: Gender and the Hollywood Detective Film*, observes that not only does Nancy own her own car, "but, even when she is with her father, she is still the one who does the driving" (78). This demonstrates an independence and self-sufficiency that were unusual at the time.

The first Nancy Drew film series, starring Bonita Granville, was quite successful and included *Nancy Drew, Detective* (William Clemens, 1938), *Nancy Drew, Reporter* (William Clemens, 1939), *Nancy Drew, Trouble Shooter* (William Clemens, 1939), and *Nancy Drew and the Hidden Staircase* (William Clemens, 1939). With a cinematic disempowerment that foreshadowed *V. I. Warshawski* decades later, Drew, as portrayed by Granville, appears younger and less capable than she is made to seem in the books. In the opening sequence for *Nancy Drew and the*

Hidden Staircase, for example, the journalists confuse the Drew family housekeeper (Renie Riano) with Nancy, making it all the more startling just how young Nancy seems. Also, in marked contrast to her literary counterpart, when Granville-as-Nancy tags along with the ice deliveryman in order to follow a lead in *Nancy Drew and the Hidden Staircase*, she complains that his job is not suitably genteel. These early movie versions also depict a version of Nancy who is more prone to wide eyes and a breathy voice. In contrast, the original Nancy was not afraid to get her hands dirty. This shift reflects how troublesome a confident female private eye can be—even when underage—and the steps Hollywood will take to make her less threatening than an adult, professional, female private eye.

Regardless of the format—silver screen or written page—Nancy manages to balance femininity with bold adventure, glamorous and interesting enough to inspire and entertain but not so glamorous and interesting that she might cause trouble. Her child status prevents her from appearing too revolutionary for several reasons. One, with her father providing financial security, Nancy does not need to worry about paying bills, and as such, her lighthearted escapades offer "pure escapism" (Mason 13, 15), both for her and for her fans. The fact that sleuthing is more a hobby than a career also liberates Nancy from another set of expectations and responsibilities. Even though she may get paid for some of her services, she is still very much an amateur whose detective prowess can be seen as a lark. When she succeeds, like Agatha Christie's Miss Marple, J. B. Fletcher (Angela Lansbury) from *Murder, She Wrote* (CBS, 1984–1996), or any other famous "amateur detective," it can be dismissed as a lucky fluke.

Second, Nancy's youth allows her to sidestep the question of why marriage is not a priority. Elderly detectives, such as Marple or Fletcher, are similarly immune to this kind of pressure, having moved past the "marrying age." Nancy does not yet have to choose between marriage and a career, and as a permanent teenager, it seems she never will. She detects however and whenever she wants, free from the confines of motherhood and marriage. Whereas the adult female private eye is forced to be either "an incompetent detective" or "an inadequate woman" (K. Klein 4, 5), Nancy's childhood status renders her exempt from both. She can be *both* a competent detective and an adequate girl.

At the same time, it is clear that Nancy is not a *typical* girl. Mature beyond her years—one explanation for this is the death of her mother when Nancy was young, forcing Nancy to perform a more active role in the household—Nancy rarely needs assistance because she can do

everything herself, and she often does it better. She is at
once a child and an adult—childlike enough to get away
with her transgressions but adult enough to succeed at
them too—much as she has characteristics common to
both boys and girls. She can act coy and girly on command, just as easily as she can scale a fence or search for
treasure in a dark and dirty tunnel. She encapsulates the
two sides of the masculine/feminine binary, and she
gets away with this because she is a child. She can move
between realms (of gender, of age) that elude a typical private eye. And it is this ability to move between realms—
adult and child, boy and girl—that makes Nancy as
powerful as she is.

So if Nancy is a socially acceptable feminist combined
with cozy mystery solver, it is especially fascinating to
watch what happens when she comes to Los Angeles. In
the 2007 film *Nancy Drew*, directed by Andrew Fleming,
Nancy (Emma Roberts) and her father, Carson Drew
(Tate Donovan), move to Los Angeles so that he can
pursue a job opportunity. Of course, Nancy being Nancy,
she selects as their temporary residence a mansion formerly owned by the movie star Dehlia Draycott (Laura
Harring), who died under mysterious circumstances.
While attending Hollywood High School, Nancy devotes
the bulk of her energy to finding Draycott's child, given
up for adoption right after birth, and finding Draycott's

will, which leaves all the money to this mystery child. Dashiel Biedermeyer (Barry Bostwick) becomes a serious threat, determined to prevent Nancy from discovering the will, as well as to conceal his role in murdering Draycott. In Los Angeles, Nancy is separated from her friends Bess and George, emphasizing just how solitary her mystery-solving endeavors often are. Ned Nickerson (Max Thieriot) does visit from River Heights, and Nancy befriends a younger classmate, Corky (Josh Flitter), but they are superfluous at best. Nancy is on her own.

In this movie, Nancy, unlike Laura Holt, Honey West, Maddie Hayes, V. I. Warshawski, or Alice Vaughan, does not have a sidekick. The entire case sits on Nancy's teenage shoulders in a way that seems impossible for her older contemporaries. She zips around Los Angeles in her convertible as if she is a native, seeming entirely at home. Contrary to expectation, her childhood status actually gives her more freedom and accessibility. Not only does she not need assistance from adults, but unlike Holt, West, Hayes, Warshawski, and Vaughan, she also seems thoroughly impervious to the needs or demands of men. She defies the men (her father, her boyfriend) who try to tell her how to behave, and she does not need their assistance to get the job done. No one—and certainly not the men in her life—is able to prevent Nancy from being Nancy.

VERONICA MARS: THE TV SHOW

Many of the terms by which I describe Nancy Drew would also apply to another girl sleuth: Veronica Mars. Veronica, the title character of the television show created by Rob Thomas, brought Nancy Drew and the girl sleuth into the twenty-first century, inspiring books (although not as many), as well as four seasons of a television show (UPN/CW, 2004–2006; Hulu, 2019), a movie, *Veronica Mars* (Rob Thomas, 2014), and a web spin-off (CW Seed, *Play It Again, Dick*).

The show was well aware of its lineage. In the show's episode "You Think You Know Somebody" (UPN, October 26, 2004), Logan Echolls (Jason Dohring)—described as the "obligatory psychotic jackass" in that same episode—tells Veronica (Kristen Bell) that she sucks "at this Nancy Drew stuff." Despite Logan's comment, Veronica Mars *is* quite good at what she does.

In the episode "There's Got to Be a Morning After Pill" (CW, February 6, 2007), Keith Mars (Enrico Colantoni), Veronica's father, intentionally conceals their identities, introducing the two of them by saying, "My name is Carson Drew. This is my assistant, Nancy." Of course, Nancy was never Carson's assistant. Like Veronica, Nancy was Carson's daughter, but the message comes across loud and clear.

Formerly the sheriff of the town of Neptune, Keith Mars now runs Mars Investigations, and it is under his tutelage that teenage Veronica learns valuable skills, including how to access elite search engines, how to tell when someone is lying, and how to conduct proper surveillance techniques. The primary man in Veronica's life is her father. Much as with Nancy, there is no mother figure present—Veronica's mother disappears due to alcoholism, among other problems—and so Veronica plays a combination of wife, daughter, and, most significantly, sidekick to her father. She is heavily involved in many of her father's cases and often procures information or performs surveillance for him. The two cook for each other and joke with each other. For example, in the episode "Poughkeepsie, Tramps, and Thieves" (CW, January 30, 2007), Veronica comes home to the apartment she shares with her father and jokingly tells him, "I come home after a hard day at work, and there you are, lounging with your bonbons and your *Harper's Bazaar*. There'd better be some freshly pressed shirts in my closet, or so help me ..." This easy banter is facilitated by the fact that the two often treat each other as equals.

Veronica is a high school student at Neptune High in seasons 1 and 2 and then a college student in season 3. Throughout those seasons, she moonlights as a private detective—or, as she puts it in the episode "Silence of the

Lamb" (UPN, January 4, 2005), does "favors for friends."
Occasionally, she charges; but she seems willing to accept
trade as a substitute for payment, and she also seems very
quick to waive the fee if the person requesting her services
cannot afford to pay it.

In the time period before the show began, Veronica had
been one of the "popular kids," part of the millionaires, or
so we are told via flashback, aided by her father's status
as sheriff, her friendship with the popular girl Lilly Kane
(Amanda Seyfried), and her relationship with Lilly's
brother, Duncan (Teddy Dunn). Unfortunately, after a
breakup with Duncan, Lilly's murder, and Keith Mars's
removal from his position as sheriff, Veronica's status
plummets. Instead of joining another group, she remains
a loner, moving between various types of students but
always remaining on her own. Even when she starts dat-
ing Duncan again, she is never really part of his group,
referred to as the "oh-niners" because of their upscale zip
code. If anything, her alienation is even more obvious in
season 2 because her rekindled intimacy with Duncan
places her in consistent contact with the oh-niners, most
of whom despise Veronica and poke fun at her impover-
ished status. She does not play their social games. Instead,
she chooses to speak her mind, and they do not like that.

If high school Veronica is the private detective for the
twenty-first century—or, at the very least, an updated

version of an old favorite—it is significant that both critics and viewers generally regard the first season of the
show as the best. In that season, she is more of a tomboy
and quite young—only a junior in high school. Her looks
and attitude make it evident that she is not just "one of the
girls," and this is reinforced by her total lack of concern
for what others think about her. In addition to the benefits afforded by her loner status, her age is frequently an
ally as well, allowing her to commit such transgressions as
sneaking information out of the police station or breaking
into the high school principal's file cabinet. She frequently
gets away with things that would get a working professional penalized. Female detectives seem to be granted
liberties when they are either very young or very old.

Ironically, Kristen Bell told *IndieWire* in 2017 that she
and creator Rob Thomas want to bring Mars back as a
miniseries: "We are willing to put the effort in. I mean,
if I have to do it as *Murder, She Wrote* at 80, we're going to
do it. It's going to happen" (qtd. in L. Miller). Bell jumps
from the one age at which female detectives can detect
with impunity (childhood) to the next age at which they
have similar freedom from "female responsibilities" such
as marriage and child rearing (retirement), skipping the
decades in between, when her freedom might be cur-
tailed. Further reinforcing the *Murder, She Wrote–Veronica
Mars* connection, in the *Veronica Mars* movie, Vinnie Van

Lowe (Ken Marino) refers to Veronica as "Neptune's very own Angela Lansbury." On *Murder, She Wrote*, Lansbury, as Jessica Fletcher, often got away with maneuvers that might get a police officer or a professional fired. After all, she was just an amateur.

As a teenager unhindered by the sexist expectations that plague older, professional, female private eyes, Veronica, much like Nancy Drew, successfully solves mysteries—usually on her own—in her fictional hometown of Neptune, a small beachside community an hour or two south of Los Angeles. Unlike Nancy, however, not all of these mysteries are charmingly self-contained or benign. Instead, as Veronica describes via voice-over in the episode "An Echolls Family Christmas" (UPN, December 14, 2004), "Christmas in Neptune is, was, and always will be about the trappings. The lights and the tinsel they use to cover up the sordidness, the corruption. No, Veronica, there is no Santa Claus," she tells herself. In the episode "Rashard and Wallace Go to White Castle" (UPN, February 1, 2006), Veronica's best friend, Wallace (Percy Daggs III), asks her if there is anyone she does not think "is corrupt deep down." Her answer is, "Yes, you." When Veronica returns to Neptune in the film, the corruption and incompetence has only intensified, and when she describes Neptune as a "seedy beach town," she is being generous.

In this respect, Veronica shares more with Marlowe and
Rawlins than with Nancy, and Neptune shares more with
Los Angeles than River Heights ever did. While some of
the cases are compact and solvable within an episode—
involving scenarios with high school bullies, suspicious
neighbors, missing parents, or a lost car—more complex
mysteries weave their way through entire seasons as befits
a true hard-boiled private eye. Many of the problems that
plague Neptune—and fill Veronica's time—link directly
to an endless web of corruption. It is clear that, even when
one case is solved, there are many more left open, and
these cases would be right at home with either Marlowe
or Rawlins at the helm.

Another way in which Veronica flexes her Marlowe-like
abilities is when she moves back and forth between the
two extremes of Neptune: the very rich and the very
poor, both of whom are her clients. Or, as she herself
says in a voice-over during the pilot episode (UPN,
September 22, 2004) as the camera pans over Neptune
High, "This is my school. If you go here, your parents are
either millionaires, or your parents work for millionaires.
Neptune, California, a town without a middle class." In
her convertible—a Chrysler LeBaron—Veronica, like
Nancy, zips all over town, confident in whatever demo-
graphic she enters.

The problems of class conflict in Neptune are exacerbated by corruption and incompetence in the sheriff's department. In the movie, Veronica manages to film the sheriff admitting that he does not care about evidence. If he thinks someone should be guilty, that is good enough for him. Much like in *The Shield*, the sheriff's department is not above planting or faking evidence in order to apprehend its desired suspects. Veronica repeatedly has to compensate for the sheriff's department's sloppy work. For example, in the episode "Plan B" (UPN, April 5, 2006), Veronica hands Balboa County's Sheriff Lamb (Michael Muhney) some crucial evidence that she has obtained, explaining that it is to steer him "in the right direction." She takes a beat and then corrects herself, acknowledging that she is, in fact, doing his job for him.

Veronica's propensity to "tell it like it is" extends beyond her interactions with authority figures. Veronica frequently provides voice-overs for viewers, and in so doing, she claims ownership over her story. It is her voice that takes us through her many adventures. A popular device for many a noir film, the use of voice-over conveys agency and authority. Much like with Nancy, no one—and certainly not the men in her life—is able to prevent Veronica from being Veronica. It is this determination that creates a central struggle between Veronica and Logan, whose on-again/off-again relationship drives much of the show's later seasons, as well as the film.

Logan, in particular, has issues with Veronica's detecting. For example, in the episode "Lord of the Pi's" (CW, November 21, 2006), the conflict over Veronica's choices comes to a climax. Logan, worried about Veronica's lack of concern for her own personal safety, hires a security guard to keep an eye on her. When she discovers what he has done, she is irate. "You had no right to do that," she tells him. He replies that he does not care if she is angry. All he cares about is that she is safe, but Veronica is unrelenting. "It's not like this is all some new facet of my personality," she declares. "You know who I am! You know what I do." Clearly, who she is and what she does will not change, regardless of Logan's preferences. If Logan cannot accept that this is who she is, then their relationship will not work.

It soon becomes clear that the issue is not as simple as the fact that Veronica frequently puts herself in harm's way. In the episode "Spit & Eggs" (CW, November 28, 2006), Logan tells her that she does not have to work so hard, to which Veronica replies, "Sure I do." Veronica likes to work hard. She does not operate any other way. As Logan breaks up with Veronica, he reminds her that she has told him that she is not "built" to let people help her. "And you know what?" he continues. "I'm not built to stand on the sidelines." Regardless, he reassures her that he will always be there for her, if she needs anything. Except, as he says bitterly, she is Veronica Mars and, therefore, never needs anything, at least not from him. Logan is right. When she does need help, she reaches out most frequently to her father or Wallace—rarely to Logan, which leaves him on the sidelines, from where he must watch Veronica and her father being true partners.

In the "Spit & Eggs" episode, when Veronica thinks she has identified a potential rape victim, Logan insists that she stay at the party, letting him go track down the rapist: "Veronica, please let me do this part." Interestingly, he does not suggest coming with her but, rather, going *instead* of her. He prefers for her to stay while he puts himself in possible danger. He is less interested in working together than in diminishing her role entirely. His frustration with how she chooses to spend her time becomes evident in a voice mail during the episode "There's Got to Be a Morning After Pill" (CW, February 6, 2007). Leaving a message, Logan asks, "So where are you, Veronica? Out digging through someone's trash maybe? Interrogating one of your friends? Beating out a confession? You know, if you dig deep enough, you're gonna find that everyone's a sinner. Judge not, Veronica."

The two rekindle their romance in the film, but only after Keith Mars is hospitalized. With him out of the way,

Veronica has more space in her life, as well as needing Logan's help because her father is absent. Bringing her home from the hospital, Logan carries her up the path and over the threshold, as if they were newlyweds. That night is the first time they have kissed in almost a decade. The next day, she asks him to come with her, to help her connect Gia (Krysten Ritter) and Luke (Sam Huntington) to the crime. She asks him for help because her father and Wallace are not available. Finally, Logan is more of a sidekick and colleague rather than exiled to the sidelines. This brings Veronica and Logan closer together, an intimacy facilitated by her need for assistance. Interestingly, Logan is now a US Navy pilot lieutenant, a position that requires tours of duty. The implication may be that it is precisely those tours of duty that allow the relationship to survive, making it easier for Veronica to juggle the two men in her life. The limited-episode return of *Veronica Mars* (to Hulu in 2019) may reveal the success of this strategy.

A crucial difference not only between Veronica and Marlowe but between Veronica and virtually every hard-boiled P.I. is her proficiency with computers and, specifically, the internet. Unlike most private eyes—for whom technology is often something to be outsourced—Veronica is adept at finding almost anything online, as befits a girl growing up at the end of the twentieth century and the start of the twenty-first. For instance, when asked if she can find a stolen car over the internet, in the episode "You Think You Know Somebody" (UPN, October 26, 2004), she replies, "You'd be surprised what one can find with a few nimble keystrokes." At the same time, as a nod to the private eye archetype, Veronica does have Cindy "Mac" Mackenzie (Tina Majorino), a computer expert to whom she turns when she has especially complicated needs. In the episode "Nevermind the Buttocks" (UPN, April 18, 2006), Mac clarifies that she does "the gadgets," while Veronica handles "the actual espionage." In the episode "Ahoy, Mateys" (UPN, November 22, 2005), Veronica refers to Mac as "Q," and Mac refers to Veronica as "Mr. Bond." "Q," an abbreviation of "Quartermaster," refers to the head of "Q Branch" or "Q Division," the research and development department that supplies Bond with tech-savvy gadgets. Q is a character that is traditionally masculine, much like Bond, and Rob Thomas subverts gender expectations by making both female. Interestingly, in the original concept for the show, the main character was male. As Thomas developed the script, however, he decided to change the protagonist's gender because "a noir piece told from a female point of view is more interesting and unique" (qtd. in Byrne).

While a noir piece told from a female point of view is certainly unique, and a noir piece told from the perspective of a female private eye is both unique and fraught with difficulty, a noir piece told from the point of view of a female child is far more than interesting or unique. Despite the fact that the creators of Nancy Drew did not want to "encourage revolution" or that Thomas claims he was merely going for a unique point of view with his choice of gender, the radical potential of a girl sleuth should not be underestimated. Her very status as "girl" allows her to pursue sleuthing in ways denied the more adult, female private eye, and by pursuing sleuthing, she pursues information, transgresses boundaries, and forms her own narrative. Ironically, the successful girl private eye seems much more attainable than the idea of a lady dick.

In certain significant moments, Veronica is referred to in gender-neutral terms or in ways that are not typically feminine, as if to acknowledge the complexities of gender and the private eye. For instance, in "The Girl Next Door" (UPN, November 9, 2004), Keith, urging Veronica to quit detective work, tells her that he wants her to have "a future as a highly paid Ivy League–educated executive of some sort who never thinks about private investigation again in her perfect life," a comment that appears remarkably non-gender-specific. Similarly, in the episode "Like a Virgin" (UPN, November 23, 2004), Meg Manning (Alona Tal) tells Veronica that she "was looking for a white horse." Veronica replies, "Oh, so now I'm your knight in shining armor?" Again, gender is neutral if not overtly masculine. In the episode "Welcome Wagon" (CW, October 3, 2006), after Veronica does a Clint Eastwood imitation, Logan retorts by saying, "I really shouldn't have pushed for the Clint Eastwood marathon. Now I've ruined you. Didn't think it was possible to make you more butch. Stupid, stupid Logan! Well, wanna feel like a man, walk me to class?" Veronica replies by asking, "Carry your books?" A few episodes later, in the episode "Spit & Eggs," Veronica says, via voice-over, "Maybe I should get into the spirit of doing things normal girlfriends do. I should make more of an effort to please my man. First come sexy underthings." Veronica says this but still does not purchase any sexy underthings.

However atypical Veronica might be, there is no question that she is significantly more feminine, at least in appearance, in season 3 than in season 1. As she grows older, her appearance becomes more traditionally feminine. Perhaps Nancy's secret for longevity might be connected to her refusal to age? In contrast, as Veronica grows older, her choppy bob from season 1 is replaced in season 3 by flat-ironed hair and bangs or, alternately, by soft, romantic waves. Rather than appearing as a punky high schooler, college Veronica frequently looks as if she is on her way to a job interview. Her hair gets longer, softer, and fuller, while her makeup gets heavier and her relationship to detecting becomes increasingly complicated. Significantly, in season 3, in addition to all the other changes—including a more "mature" opening credit sequence—the LeBaron convertible is replaced with a Saturn VUE, a compact sport utility vehicle without a retractable roof. Perhaps Veronica loses her special powers as she matures?

VERONICA MARS: THE FILM

As previously explained, there are many difficulties inherent in being an adult female private eye. Despite the progressive nature of the television series, the *Veronica Mars* movie, in particular, acknowledges some of these difficulties. When Veronica gets older, rather than forging a new path—redefining what the adult female private eye can be—she appears increasingly uncomfortable with this kind of work. The most noticeable example in the film is the repeated comparisons between her work as a detective and addiction. Veronica makes the comparison over and over, not only comparing detective work to a weakness, a vice, and a compulsion but also specifically comparing it to her own mother's alcoholism.

Significantly, in the film's opening voice-over, Veronica begins by diminishing her initial pull toward detective work. She explains that she knows how dumb "a teenaged private eye" sounds but that it is not as if she "found a decoder ring at the bottom of a cereal box and thought, 'that sounds like fun.'" Instead, Veronica begins her detective work after her high school best friend is murdered, trying to discover who killed her. Her initial drive comes from grief and a sense of responsibility, much like Honey West and V. I. Warshawski. She needs to clean up the mess because no one else will do it, not because she is especially talented or because public pressure demands it.

Fast-forward a decade, and recent law-school graduate Veronica is interviewing at a prestigious New York law firm. When she is asked about her detective experiences, Veronica further minimizes the work she did as a detective, dismissing it as merely "answering phones" and handling her father's travel. The lawyers interviewing her press harder, pointing out that she is mentioned on LexisNexis in fifteen separate articles or briefs, "in cases ranging from multiple homicides to dognapping." Again, Veronica dismisses her accomplishments, attributing them to compulsive behavior and an addictive personality, possibly connected to being an "adrenaline junkie." She then explains that she is no longer a detective because the price was too high: "it ruined friendships and relationships." Now that she is older and more mature, those friendships and relationships take priority.

In the film, Veronica unexpectedly heads back to Neptune, to help Logan, who has been wrongfully accused of murder. Once again, she feels the pull and sense of responsibility. She emphasizes that this compulsion does not come from a place of talent or skill but, rather, from weakness and addiction. She asks herself, as she looks through her old detective gear, "Hasn't your life been better since giving this up?" It is unclear, however, in what ways her life has been better. "Everything you worked for is right in front of you," she reminds herself. "Solid relationship. Quality job prospects. A low-profile existence. Or does all that just bore the shit out of you, Veronica?" That might sound superficially convincing, but the "solid relationship" quickly disintegrates once Veronica is back in Neptune, the primary appeal of the "quality job prospects" is only that they will allow Veronica to pay off her student loans, and the benefits of a "low-profile existence" are never explained. Nonetheless, she and her father seem convinced that becoming a detective in Neptune would basically be giving up and ceding power to her addiction.

This internal conflict continues throughout the film, with the "addiction" metaphor repeated over and over. When Veronica begins helping Logan find the actual killer, she reassures herself that it is only "a one-time deal, a farewell tour, if you will," before being forced to acknowledge that a junkie is never satisfied with "one more taste of the good stuff." Once she has convinced herself that she *is* going back to New York, to start at her new law firm on

Monday, she basks in the self-congratulations: "Do I get a chip for this? Pouring the drink, swishing it, smelling it, leaving the bar without taking a sip. Is this what getting clean feels like?" Of course, drugs and Veronica being what they are, she does not head back to New York, choosing instead to delve deeper into Neptune's corruption.

Veronica, at her high school reunion's "after-party," tells viewers, via voice-over, that while it looks like she is having fun, even her "alkie mom knew how to put on a show to hide her disease. She could PTA with the best of them, but her mind was never far from that bit of liquid courage she kept handy." Again, the drive to pursue truth and expose criminality is compared to a disease. When her father recognizes that Veronica might be staying in Neptune—rather than returning to her life in New York—he tells her, "You did it, kid. You made it out. Don't let this town take you down, like it does everyone else." But his protestations are in vain. Veronica is unable to kick her "addiction," and by the end of the movie, she has resigned herself to this impasse:

So what now? I had a ringside seat to my mom's recovery attempts. I know all about accepting the things I can't change. I'm supposed to find the courage to change the things I can, even if it means disappointing the one man I can't bear to disappoint. . . . If I were wise enough to know the difference, between what I can and can't change, would I even be who I am? . . . I've rolled around in the mud for so long. Wash me clean, and I don't recognize myself. So how about I just accept the mud and the tendency I have to find myself rolling in it. My name is Veronica, and I'm an addict.

The movie's stance on detective proclivities is clear. Rather than Veronica's being acknowledged for her brilliant mind and keen powers of deduction (as frequently accompanies Sherlock Holmes's revelations, for instance), her talents are not merely ignored or dismissed but literally equated with a disease, with a vice, with an unhealthy compulsion. Rather than presenting her return to private investigation as empowering, this decision is depicted as a failure to improve herself. This choice, on the part of the team behind the movie, is an interesting—albeit disappointing—one. The film could have presented Veronica as returning to her roots, reconnecting with her true self, realizing that the façade of "conservative adulthood" was not for her and that, instead, she should forge her own path, even if it means disappointing cultural and social expectations.

At one point, near the end of the film, Keith Mars says, imitating Charlie Chan—a fictional police detective for the Honolulu Police Department created by Earl Derr Biggers and starring in books, movies, and even television shows—"When number-one daughter was young, her skills were sharp, like blade of sword. Now . . . brain dull, like blade of plow." The more Veronica outgrows the label of "girl sleuth," the more something shifts with her, and it is more complex than simply dulling the brain. Although Veronica does solve the primary case in the movie, clearing Logan's name in the process, her attitude toward detecting has changed. It is no longer something of which she is proud but, rather, something to which she cedes control. She gives up trying to be a "better person" and resigns herself to a life of addiction as a Neptune private investigator. This supposed regression is further reinforced by the song used for the film's closing credits—"We Used to Be Friends," by The Dandy Warhols—the same song used for the opening credits of seasons 1 and 2. For season 3, the show opted for a more "adult" version of the opening credits.

Setting Veronica Mars in the town of Neptune, much like Nancy's River Heights, works well from a narrative standpoint, or at least it did in the beginning. As creator Rob Thomas explains, "I had a 17 year old girl who was going to be fucking with the town's corrupt power structure, and I felt it was more believable in a small beach community than in a big city." Originally, Thomas planned to set the show north of Los Angeles, in a fictionalized Santa Barbara or Ventura, before settling on

San Diego as a result of a union deal. The location did not matter much, as long as it was an hour or two outside Los Angeles. The small town provides Veronica with power and opportunity that might elude her in a big-city setting, while still leaving her close enough to reach Los Angeles easily by car. However, the awkwardness of the film's reconciliation of Veronica's older age with her return to her Neptune roots makes one wonder, can Veronica only detect in Neptune? What would happen, for instance, if she moved an hour or two north to Los Angeles? Interestingly, a season 4 of *Veronica Mars* was pitched to the CW network, with the premise being "Veronica Mars as FBI agent." Based on precedent, women detectives, after all—unlike girls—work best with teams and partners, so the move makes sense. However, the network passed on it. The awkwardness of making Veronica Mars—fiercely independent and precocious sleuth—just another "G-man" is evident in the season 4 trailer.

PRIVATE EYES

While Veronica circa 2014 had not yet graduated to "big-city crime," the town of Neptune shows us two things: one, that small towns can also be wracked with crime, conspiracy, and corruption; and two, that the private detective's primary appeal comes not from the fast-paced forensics-heavy crime solving we expect from shows such as *CSI* (CBS, 2000–2015) or from the formula-rich predictability of *Law & Order: SVU* (NBC, 1999–present) or from the rough and raw antics on *The Shield* (FX, 2002–2008)—all those elements are, in fact, remarkably absent from *Veronica Mars*—but, rather, from the simple storytelling of good versus bad, depictions of the power of perseverance and conviction. The L.A. private eye, whether Veronica as "L.A. private eye in training" or any of the others, demonstrates the power of the individual. In a society and a city where individuality feels increasingly anonymous and powerless, there is affirmation to watching a solitary person acting—with no ulterior motive—to make things right.

As our lives appear more and more online, as it becomes easier to share and to observe, we have all become private eyes. However, this does not negate the need for— or the appeal of—the professional private eye, despite the consistently flawed depictions that persist. If anything, we can see through Veronica Mars just how the trope can and must evolve, as well as its increasing relevance in a world where we drown in information overload, much of it redundant, useless, or ephemeral. If the pleasure of the detective narrative comes from watching the detective pursue this information, the skill of the private eye has always come from knowing which information to follow and which to ignore. We need the private eye to make sense of the private, to sift through the white noise, and to expose that which is hidden, to make connections we cannot see, to discover what we cannot find on our own.

ACKNOWLEDGMENTS

My thanks to Leslie Mitchner for "tricking" me into writing this book, to Melody for putting up with me, to Tom for the scans and the reading lists, and to my father for recording those Sherlock Holmes episodes on cassette way back when. I would also like to thank Nicole Solano of Rutgers University Press and Quick Takes series editors Gwendolyn Audrey Foster and Wheeler Winston Dixon for believing in this project. Thank you, as well, to Andrew Katz, for the careful scrutiny; Toby Miller, for sharing my love of private eyes; and Stephen Tropiano, for the constant support. This book was written under the supervision of Tandy Philip Franciosa, and for that I am grateful.

FURTHER READING

Baker, Robert A., and Michael T. Nietzel. *Private Eyes: One Hundred and One Knights.* Bowling Green, OH: Bowling Green State University Popular Press, 1985.

Chandler, Raymond. *The Big Sleep; Farewell, My Lovely; The High Window.* New York: Knopf, 2002.

Fine, David. *Imagining Los Angeles.* Reno: University of Nevada Press, 2004.

Gates, Philippa. *Detecting Men: Masculinity and the Hollywood Detective Film.* Albany: State University of New York Press, 2006.

Klein, Kathleen Gregory. *The Woman Detective: Gender and Genre.* Urbana: University of Illinois Press, 1988.

Mason, Bobbie Ann. *The Girl Sleuth: A Feminist Guide.* Old Westbury, NY: Feminist Press, 1975.

McShane, Frank. *The Life of Raymond Chandler.* New York: Penguin Books, 1979.

Mizejewski, Linda. *Hardboiled & High Heeled: The Woman Detective in Popular Culture.* New York: Routledge, 2004.

Mosley, Walter. *Black Betty.* New York: Norton, 1994.

Most, Glenn W., and William W. Stowe, eds. *The Poetics of Murder: Detective Fiction and Literary Theory.* New York: Harcourt, 1983.

Nichol, Bran. *The Private Eye: Detectives in the Movies*. London: Reaktion Books, 2013.

Porter, Dennis. *The Pursuit of Crime: Art and Ideology in Detective Fiction*. New Haven, CT: Yale University Press, 1981.

Walton, John. *The Legendary Detective: The Private Eye in Fact and Fiction*. Chicago: University of Chicago Press, 2015.

WORKS CITED

Alewyn, Richard. "The Origin of the Detective Novel." *The Poetics of Murder*. Ed. Glenn W. Most and William W. Stowe. San Diego: Harcourt Brace Jovanovich, 1983. 62–78.

Andrews, Evan. "What Were the Zoot Suit Riots?" *History .com* 18 Nov. 2015. Web. http://www.history.com/news/ ask-history/what-were-the-zoot-suit-riots.

Baker, Robert A., and Michael T. Nietzel. *Private Eyes: One Hundred and One Knights*. Bowling Green, OH: Bowling Green State University Popular Press, 1985.

Bennetts, Leslie. "Beautiful People, Ugly Choices." *Vanity Fair* Sept. 2009. Web. https://www.vanityfair.com/ culture/2009/09/farrah-fawcett200909.

Berardinelli, James. "Devil in a Blue Dress," *ReelViews*. Web. 20 Sept. 2017. http://www.reelviews.net/reelviews/ devil-in-a-blue-dress.

Berger, Roger. "'The Black Dick': Race, Sexuality, and Discourse in the L.A. Novels of Walter Mosley." *African American Review* 31.2 (1997): 281–294.

Bleakley, Amy, Patrick E. Jamieson, and Daniel Romer. "Trends of Sexual and Violent Content by Gender in Top-Grossing U.S. Films, 1950–2006." *Journal of Adolescent Health* 51.1 (2012): 73–79.

Bould, Mark. *Film Noir: From Berlin to Sin City*. London: Wallflower, 2005.

Browne, Ray B. *Heroes and Humanities: Detective Fiction and Culture*. Bowling Green, OH: Bowling Green State University Popular Press, 1986.

Byrne, Bridget. "Clash of Cultures Drives 'Veronica Mars.'" *Orange County Register* 22 Sept. 2004. Web. https://web.archive.org/web/20071230010222/http://www.ocregister.com/ocr/sections/entertainment/et_television/article_248468.php.

Caron, Glenn Gordon. "Memories of Moonlighting." *Moonlighting—Season 3*. Lions Gate Entertainment. 2006. DVD.

Cawelti, John. "*Chinatown* and Generic Transformation in Recent American Films." *Film Genre Reader IV*. Ed. Barry Keith Grant. Austin: University of Texas Press, 2012. 279–297.

Coursodon, Jean-Pierre. "Arthur Penn." *Arthur Penn: Interviews*. Ed. Michael Chaiken and Paul Cronin. Jackson: University Press of Mississippi, 2008. 111–132.

Chandler, Raymond. *The Big Sleep; Farewell, My Lovely; The High Window*. New York: Knopf, 2002.

———. "Casual Notes on the Mystery Novel." *Raymond Chandler Speaking*. Ed. Dorothy Gardiner and Kathrine Sorley Walker. Berkeley: University of California Press, 1997. 63–70.

———. "Chandler on His Novels, Short Stories, and Philip Marlowe." *Raymond Chandler Speaking*. Ed. Dorothy Gardiner and Kathrine Sorley Walker. Berkeley: University of California Press, 1997. 205–250.

———. "Letter to Jamie Hamilton." 21 Mar. 1949. *The Raymond Chandler Papers: Selected Letters and Nonfiction 1909–1959*. Ed. Tom Hiney and Frank Macshane. New York: Grove, 2000. 105.

———. *The Big Sleep*. New York: Vintage Crime / Black Lizard. 1966.

———. *The Long Goodbye*. New York: Ballantine Books, 1973.

———. *The Notebooks of Raymond Chandler*. New York: HarperCollins, 1976.

———. "The Simple Art of Murder." *Raymond Chandler: Later Novels and Other Writings*. New York: Library of America, 1995. 977–992.

———. "Twelve Notes on the Mystery Story." *Later Novels and Other Writings*. New York: Library of America, 1995. 1004–1011.

Christie, Agatha. *Poirot's Early Cases*. London: HarperCollins, 2016.

Clarens, Carlos. *Crime Movies: An Illustrated History*. New York: Norton, 1980.

Daly, Carroll John. *The Snarl of the Beast*. New York: Edward J. Clode, 1927.

Dimendberg, Edward. *Film Noir and the Spaces of Modernity*. Cambridge, MA: Harvard University Press, 2004.

Eaton, Michael. *Chinatown*. London: BFI, 1997.

Farber, Manny. *Negative Space: Manny Farber on the Movies*. New York: Da Capo, 1998.

Felsenthal, Julia. "*The Catch* Is Shondaland's Take on a Soft-Boiled Caper." *Vogue* 23 Mar. 2016. Web. https://www.vogue.com/article/the-catch-abc-review.

Fine, David, *Imagining Los Angeles*. Reno: University of Nevada Press, 2004.

Gates, Philippa. *Detecting Men: Masculinity and the Hollywood Detective Film*. Albany: State University of New York Press, 2006.

Glover, David. "The Stuff That Dreams are Made of: Masculinity, Femininity, and the Thriller." *Gender, Genre, and Narrative Pleasure*. Ed. Derek Longhurst. London: Routledge, 2012. 67–83.

Hamilton, Denise. *The Last Embrace*. New York: Scribner, 2008.

Hammett, Dashiell. *The Maltese Falcon*. New York: Vintage Crime / Black Lizard, 1992.

Hirsch, Foster. *Detours and Lost Highways: A Map of Neo-Noir*. New York: Proscenium, 1999.

Holloway, Daniel. "New 2017–2018 TV Shows Are Mostly White and Male." *Variety* 19 May 2017. Web. http://variety.com/2017/tv/news/new-2017-18-tv-shows-no-diversity-1202436493/.

Irwin, John. *Unless the Threat of Death Is Behind Them: Hard-Boiled Fiction and Film Noir*. Baltimore: Johns Hopkins University Press, 2006.

Jameson, Frederic. *Raymond Chandler: The Detections of Totality*. London: Verso, 2016.

Jenner, Mareike. "The Detective Series." *The Television Genre Book*. 3rd ed. Ed. Glen Creeber. London: BFI, 2018.

Klein, Kathleen Gregory. *The Woman Detective: Gender and Genre*. Urbana: University of Illinois Press, 1988.

Klein, Norman M. *The History of Forgetting: Los Angeles and the Erasure of Memory*. London York: Verso, 2003.

Lewis, Jon. *Hard-Boiled Hollywood: Crime and Punishment in Postwar Los Angeles*. Berkeley: University of California Press, 2017.

Malnic, Eric. "The Aqueduct: DWP Smoothes Out Rough Edges on 74-Year-Old Engineering Marvel." *L.A. Times* 18 Oct. 1987. Web. http://articles.latimes.com/1987-10-18/local/me-15046_1_los-angeles-river.

Margolies, Edward. *Which Way Did He Go? The Private Eye in Dashiell Hammett, Raymond Chandler, Chester Himes, and Ross Macdonald*. New York: Holmes and Meier, 1982.

Mason, Bobbie Ann. *The Girl Sleuth: A Feminist Guide*. Old Westbury, NY: Feminist Press, 1975.

Maxfield, James. "'The Injustice of It All': Polanski's Revision of the Private Eye Genre in *Chinatown*." *The Detective in American Fiction, Film, and Television*. Ed. Jerome H. Delamater and Ruth Prigozy. Westport, CT: Greenwood, 1998. 93–102.

McLellan, Dennis. "Skip Fickling, Honey West Creator, Dies." *Los Angeles Times* 11 Apr. 1998. Web. http://articles.latimes.com/1998/apr/11/local/me-38189.

McShane, Frank. *The Life of Raymond Chandler*. New York: Penguin Books, 1979.

Miller, Daniel. "Finding Marlowe." *Los Angeles Times* 1 Nov. 2014. Web. http://graphics.latimes.com/finding-marlowe/.

Miller, Liz Shannon. "'Veronica Mars': Kristen Bell Says a New Miniseries 'Is Going to Happen.'" *IndieWire* 25 Oct. 2017. Web. http://www.indiewire.com/2017/10/veronica-mars-new-miniseries-kristen-bell-ryan-hansen-1201890834/.

Mizejewski, Linda. *Hardboiled and High Heeled: The Woman Detective in Popular Culture*. New York: Routledge, 2004.

Monk-Turner, Elizabeth, Homer Martinez, Jason Holbrook, and Nathan Harvey. "Are Reality TV Crime Shows Continuing to Perpetuate Crime Myths?" *Internet Journal of Criminology* 2007. Web. http://citeseerx.ist.psu.edu/viewdoc/download?doi=10.1.1.601.7250&rep=rep1&type=pdf.

Mosley, Walter. *Black Betty*. New York: Norton, 1994.

———. "The Black Dick." *Critical Fictions: The Politics of Imaginative Writing*. Ed. Philomena Mariani. Seattle: Bay, 1991. 131–133.

———. *Charcoal Joe: An Easy Rawlins Mystery*. New York: Vintage Books, 2016.

Nichol, Bran. *The Private Eye: Detectives in the Movies*. London: Reaktion Books, 2013.

Nicolson, Marjorie Hope. "The Professor and the Detective." *The Art of the Mystery Story*. Ed. Howard Haycraft. New York: Simon and Schuster, 1946. 110–127.

Paretsky, Sara. *Indemnity Only*. New York: Dell, 1982.

Poe, Edgar Allan. "The Murders in the Rue Morgue." *Tales of Mystery, Imagination, & Humour and Poems*. Cambridge: Cambridge University Press, 2013. 80–121.

Polanski, Roman. *Roman by Polanski*. New York: William Morrow, 1984.

Porter, Dennis. "Backward Construction and the Art of Suspense." *The Poetics of Murder: Detective Fiction and Literary Theory*. Ed. Glenn W. Most and William W. Stowe. New York: Harcourt, 1983. 327–340.

———. *The Pursuit of Crime: Art and Ideology in Detective Fiction*. New Haven, CT: Yale University Press, 1981.

Ransil, Louise. Message to the author. 29 Dec. 2017. E-mail.

Sampson, Henry. *Blacks in Black and White: A Source Book on Black Films*. Metuchen, NJ: Scarecrow, 1995.

Shklovsky, Victor. "The Connection between Devices of Syuzhet Construction and General Stylistic Devices." 1919. *Russian Formalism: A Collection of Articles and Texts in Translation*. Ed. Stephen Bann and John E. Bowet. Edinburgh: Scottish Academic Press, 1973. 48–72.

Shuker-Haines, Timothy, and Martha M. Umphrey. "Gender (De)Mystified: Resistance and Recuperation in Hard-Boiled Female Detective Fiction." *The Detective in American Fiction, Film, and Television*. Ed. Jerome H. Delamater and Ruth Prigozy. Westport, CT: Greenwood, 1998. 71–82.

Smith, Kevin Burton. "Honey West." *Thrilling Detective* 29 Sept. 2017. Web. http://www.thrillingdetective.com/honey.html.

Sragow, Michael. "City of Angles." *Dallas Observer* 11 Sept. 1997. Web. http://www.dallasobserver.com/film/city-of-angles-6402511.

Sumser, John. *Morality and Social Order in Television Crime Dramas*. Jefferson, NC: McFarland, 1996.

Thomas, Rob. Message to the author. 9 Jan. 2018. E-mail.

Turchiano, Danielle. "AMC, CBS, CW, Have a 'Black Problem' in Writers Rooms, New Report Finds." *Variety* 1 Nov. 2017. Web. http://variety.com/2017/tv/news/amc-cbs-cw-black-problem-writers-room-diversity-color-of-change-report-1202604594/.

Walton, John. *The Legendary Detective: The Private Eye in Fact and Fiction*. Chicago: University of Chicago Press, 2015.

Wilkerson, David. "Gangster Films of the 1930s and Their Many Levels of Fascination." *Reveal Shot* 4 Mar. 2017. Web. http://www.revealshot.com/gangster-films-of -the-1930s-and-their-many-levels-of-fascination-part-i/.

INDEX

ABOUT THE AUTHOR

Dahlia Schweitzer is an adjunct professor at Art Center College of Design in Pasadena. Her previous works include *Going Viral: Zombies, Viruses, and the End of the World* (2018), *Cindy Sherman's Office Killer: Another Kind of Monster* (2014) and essays in publications including *Cinema Journal, Journal of Popular Film and Television,* and *Journal of Popular Culture.*